Our Folk Soul
(2017)

*

an Irrational Ethic
(2017)

★

two essays

★

Traumear

The essay 'Our Folk Soul' was conceived as an exploration of what had occurred to me for some time as one of two possible ways for us to cooperate with god. My experience of human beings in community taught me that we do not all relate to god in the same way. Simply put, some come to god, others accept god. Some place the emphasis on doing, others on being and behaviour.

During the course of this exploration I made some interesting discoveries, which persuaded me, in the end, to write an Irrational Ethic, in comparison to the more lengthy exploratory essay on rational ethics I had written many years ago.

I hope the reader of these two essays will approach them with an open mind, for they are in no way intended as a contribution to traditional, western, philosophical or theological thought. They make no pretension to academic, orthodox acceptability.

*

Index of titles

*

Our Folk Soul

When we consider what it is that makes us leap into danger, without thought of harm to ourselves, to save some unfortunate creature from drowning or from whatever danger to life and limb, we soon come to the conclusion that this is not heroism or foolhardiness but rather a simple expression of the need we feel to sustain life and to aid and abet survival as much as lies in our power.

On the other hand, we are not slow to join with others in celebration of common values. When that spirit of togetherness, of decent fellowship touches us, we participate because our joy is heightened – but let a single injustice occur in our vicinity and we cannot help ourselves but we speak out. We brush aside all special considerations of fashion, custom and standing because something possibly quite unfamiliar at the time rises to the surface within us and demands our primary attention, due to a variety of reasons. It may be a case of abuse by the stronger of the weak. An individual, or even an ethnic group finds itself in difficulties, perhaps through no fault of their own, and quickly we reach out a helping hand.

What identifies the true folk-character of the compassionate action is that we do not first reckon need or weigh moral cause and consequence but we act simply. Not foolishly but simply. We know, we are certain beyond a doubt, that our interference is right, that our compassion shall be acted out; in short, that what we are about to do – or leave undone – is justified beyond justification. Afterwards we may be made to look foolish or foolish people will laud us as heroes – while we know in ourselves that we could not have behaved otherwise.

*

Even the elements conjoin on behalf of humanity. When economic calculation and political expediency outweigh personal care and attention, the balance will eventually be restored, by hook or by crook, come hell or high water. The folk-nature will assert itself, not only from within ourselves but we may equally observe it coming alive within entire populations, as outbursts of behaviour that appear on the surface as contrary to good sense – especially where good sense is liable to be misunderstood in terms of progressive society and the civilized status quo.

Let us by all means be aware of that balance which time and again establishes itself, the balance, shall we say, of the rational and the irrational, of the cerebral and the emotional, or however we like to define what happens at times whatever our best intentions. As human beings we are aware of cycles of development, of periods of evolution in reference to our individual being, and we gladly confess, especially from within our maturity, that these are commonly descriptions 'after the fact', descriptions of what happened and even of what is happening, not of what has been planned and executed.

At the same time, in addition to this periodic establishment of harmony with which the philosophers even from the time of our so-called pre-Socratics have been familiar, we refuse to remain ignorant of an unmistakable forward motion, a movement towards a point of culmination that is perhaps best described in the dynamic terms of ripeness, of growth towards fulfilment in terms of wellbeing and thriving – but on earth, not in some supernatural realm of utopian idolatry.

A favourite passive image here has always been water meandering downhill in response to gravity.

*

It is perfectly possible – and in an important sense rather wise too – to imagine a population that permanently thrives within parameters of <u>perception</u>, <u>fulfilment</u> and <u>ripeness</u>, without our having to posit subsequent decay and decline. We know that even in a modern society now and then individual human beings come to the fore and then do not decline or decay, not even during a 'ripe old age'. When they leave the earth, we know that they still exist for us as an appreciable ethical influence, by their works and in our grateful memory.

Equipped now with this twin notion of equipoise and dynamic, I return to the meaning of folk-nature and observe that here too we find ourselves in the presence of a quantity that cannot in itself be observed and that 'does not come with observation'. What counts is that we prepare for it and that we both learn and appreciate the event of its coming – which event – as we do well to countenance right from the start – is bound, at first, to occur to us as <u>uncomfortable</u>, <u>inconvenient</u> and <u>disagreeable</u>, all three at once.

Unavoidably we come upon these signs and invariably we react. Of course we do. We are not very likely to find something disagreeable, etc. and respond to it initially as though it were a pleasure, a joy or pure happiness. In fact we might as well admit that discomfort etc. is itself a reaction of ours. Reactions are automatic. Responses are intentional. This by the way.

*

The descriptive name for the combination of what we are liable to experience as uncomfortable, inconvenient and disagreeable, all three in unison, is 'reactionary forces'. That is how they arrive on our doorstep: reactively and forcefully. That is how we get the opportunity to look at them. There is no such thing as sneaking a peak before they arrive so as to be able to prevent them, in the interest of continued comfort, convenience and agreeableness. In other words, there is no 'sign' that warns us of their coming.

It is a central characteristic of this experience that we feel totally addressed. In other words, we are not in the observational presence of a peripheral appeal to our attention and we cannot simply step aside and ignore what is, in a sense, happening to us. And this is because the folk-natural character is truthful.

We either come upon it within ourselves, when we notice how we suddenly behave, or tend to behave, within our present environment, in some typically reactionary fashion, or we may come upon it in the behaviour of others, which strikes us as unusual, unpremeditated and unpredictable, all three. In sum, we are astonished, perhaps by the behaviour of an individual person, or more tellingly by the behaviour of a whole group of people; by some segment of a population.

*

So the folk-character is what we notice and what we can look at, while the folk-nature is what has this character. The fork-reality amounts to – and makes for – a corrective move forward. An understanding, in the light of day, of these characteristics allows us, as it were, to roll with the punches. For example we need to know that something irrepressible is going on. One often tragic mistake both private individuals and political leaders make is to confront an instance of folk-character as though it were a disorder which can be repressed. However an existential corrective cannot itself be corrected and any attempt to do so ends in mayhem and bloodshed. A creative human being will know what is going on in himself and will eventually learn how to 'suffer the consequences', such as feelings of guilt, shame and despondency, which will arise to the extent that 'the ground had not been prepared.' We should not suppose that a social conscience, manners and politeness can prevent such a valuable corrective to our progress if we are evolving human beings. Equally would we be foolish to insist that government policy can forestall or prevent the folk-nature of a population. Ethnic cleansing, from a practical point of view, is the height of foolishness, because the spirit of those who have been killed will ravage the souls of those who did the killing.

In the face of an outburst of folk nature, such as when a segment of the population revolts and insists on itself – which insistence can take on a great variety of appearances – an initial reaction to 'the disorder' must be turned into a response as quickly as possible. Exactly the same approach is necessary in a community or in a relationship when an individual person insists on him- or herself. The reaction happens, the response is worked out.

It is a unique characteristic, this insistence on oneself. There is a world of difference between it and an insistence on one's self, one's ego. The latter is an unfortunate miscarriage of justice, or, seen from the other side – there are always two sides to every ego – a case of mistaken identity. The one who has gone astray needs to be brought back to his or her senses, in good time, as gently as possible, though this is not always possible; much depends on circumstances. I bring up the phenomenon of insistence on one's self only so as to be able to compare the insistence on oneself to it. This is a crucial comparison and a mature mind is required for the knowing and telling of the difference. Egos 'flourish' to the detriment of all around them. I myself, however, and you yourself, we all actually need to flourish and to be able to flourish, for the wellbeing of all around us, so if circumstances act as hindrances, or if we ourselves have become inattentive to our evolution – to the way we flourish – our nature cannot help but exert itself, and this, seen from without, is then perceived correctly as folk-characteristic behaviour.

5

*

The so-called flourishing of an ego is rank in the sense of crass. My only reason for using the expression 'flourishing' even in the case of the ego is that to the egotistic one, (individual or population) it does seem that way. It is, of course, a flower that turns into bad fruit. During the past hundred years or so we have seen, across the earth, the crassest imaginable examples of national-egotistic (nationalist) rank efflorescence, loathsome behaviour by governments and populations which illustrated the unavoidable course of events in the absence of good spirit and ethical thought.

It is therefore a great pity when an outburst of folk-nature is mistaken for egotism – for individualism or nationalism.

*

What I mean by folk-nature is, of course, an aspect of human nature, however specifically in terms of human nature as evolutionary, not as developmental. We can speak sensibly of stages of development, which lead up to the so-called last stage, which is not really a stage at all because it amounts to the flowering and fruit-bearing of the mature being. We should not really refer to maturity as a stage of growth, because the end-result of growth is at stake and of the essence. So the growth-cycle is developmental, which leads up to the mature adult being. Then something new needs to be taken into consideration, which can be discussed rationally and experienced ontologically. What was principally individual becomes communal. An entirely outward influence – an influence from without and not at all from within – makes itself felt and needs to be countenanced as such. Communal responsibility is called for, not as a moral-social duty but as ethical-physical necessity. All that we do to try to sidestep this necessity, in other words flaunting our youth and losing it or flouting our maturity and losing sight of

6

it, is what makes us modern. Modernity is finally an unwilling-ness to evolve, so that development becomes exuberant and must end in decay. We have to choose to be contemporary rather than modern and we have to evolve if we are to avoid decay.

*

Wherever human nature – I mean human nature in growth – finally seeks to evolve and is ready to evolve, upon sufficient development, it is liable to announce itself as folk-natural. This is not at first dramatically evident. Nature makes no great fuss if there is no need. A need becomes evident and attention needs to be paid when modernity, as a delaying force, will not budge. So all folk-characteristics, however mildly or dramatically they present, are at least signs of good health – or better, they testify to organic strength. There is readiness for evolution. Organi-cally a quietus precedes. A period of dreamlike efflorescence seems to draw all the attention of the affected body – affected by the influence solely from without – to the change that is coming about.

*

We should not imagine that the evolution of a human being in our modern world can, even at the best of times, proceed smoothly. Modern history documents the pursuit of ideals which have in common the one element, namely arrested de-velopment. So right from the start, human development turns into a problematic issue because the modern emphasis is an economic, social and cultural development, all of which are attempts to make do with one side of the coin forever, rather than joining both sides of the equation. This is the source then of the popular spirit, negatively expressed when people rage, at times, against any protracted insistence, by 'the powers that be', on just that one side of the equation. Revolutions are there-fore reactions against one-sided development. They are symp-

7

tomatic of an imbalance. However they <u>never bring about an improvement</u>. Individual human beings must then step into the breach and take matters in hand. There are those then who have insight into the true development and also those who merely have in mind to restore the one-sided order, but this time on the other side of the divide.

The true development is advanced by those who understand that <u>development is</u> <u>not an end in itself</u>. Rivers flow into the ocean. How clear the necessity of eventual and final evolution is to those who advance development in the spirit of truth! This is another story. A critique of their work, of their clarity of vision, will tell the tale.

The simple truth of the matter is that the human spirit develops and then it evolves. It does so within human beings and this is shown in their being and in their works. Any attempt to draw a time-line of progress is hypocritical because we cannot step out of our human condition and then make truthful pronouncements about ourselves in that condition. The human condition, all else left unsaid, is after all the one that suits us best. The fact that our eventual evolution is always somehow dangled in front of us, like a carrot before the donkey, prevents us from falling entirely by the wayside. Mercifully the pain increases as we lose sight of our goal; which says nothing for those who insist they are perfectly happy behaving as if there were neither attraction nor direction that is providentially good.

*

So I distinguish between the <u>popular reaction</u> and the <u>folk-reaction</u>, the former being against one-sided development and the latter initially against evolution. Evolution, obviously, cannot be one-sided. It cannot commence until the left and the right hand cooperate in the one creative task. However just as we can get bogged down in one-sided development, so can we

8

also get stuck in development as such, as we react against the need to evolve.

Our work always begins as soon as we recognize the reaction and turn it into response; as soon as we become creative, either on the side of <u>true development</u> or in line with <u>real evolution</u>.

One aspect of our creativity will always be our willingness to help with the education of those who are stuck in reaction. Our most efficient and economical task will then be to cooperate with the corrective that already exists human-naturally but is not yet understood as such. There is the revolutionary- and the folk-corrective, both of which may be understood as functioning initially on behalf of individual human beings and eventually on behalf of community. The latter, the folk corrective, is the one that interests us especially in this essay but the comparison to symptoms of arrested development is important, so that we do not confuse the two.

*

So whatever else we mean by folk-nature and folk-character, the main meaning of it is that evolution is on the cards.

Now while true development (which is development not to its own ends but towards evolution) can make us nervous and anxious, in the modern fashion, before we submit to it, so will real evolution initially terrify us, before we give in to it or co-operate with it. The so-called terrorism, nowadays, especially in the western world, 'means' that evolution is 'making itself felt'. We are not to develop forever. That is neither natural nor organic. Nor of course can we ourselves decide when we, as persons or as humanity in general, are ready for evolution. What counts is that we do not reject our evolution when the time is ripe.

There is a flourishing of morbid art in our time, and the public cannot get enough of it, of the morbid fantasy, because it holds out a temporary promise of eternal, uninterrupted development under the terrifying pressure of evolutionary moments.

Understandably nobody likes to be rushed into anything. Nonetheless a major change is on the way and the sooner we evaluate the reactions to it in a positively creative fashion the better.

The change from development to evolution is necessarily sudden and abrupt. Very likely, at first, we haven't a notion of what has happened. Certainly we have no idea. And it takes some time to 'sink in'. There are all the physiological syndromes that could be discussed and hopefully they are dealt with creatively, with understanding. Sadly the orthodox medical profession has not yet widened its horizon, so drugs have to be prescribed to protect Society – that modern myth. I try to take care not to oversimplify here. Those who want to overcome their terror as they espouse evolution do well to count the cost. What I mean by that is: Don't be hasty. Know that if you have been chosen to evolve, nothing can permanently harm you but why make enemies? The right number of enemies will be supplied without you having to add more. Keep your ear to the ground. Don't be in a rush to join the like-minded. When the time comes for you to get down to specifics, the like-minded melt into the background and you don't want to make the mistake of misinterpreting this as a misfortune.

And learn to recognize the folk-characteristics as they crop up primarily in yourself. There is your desire to be totally honest and straightforward with those around you. If you have a tendency to wear your heart on your sleeve in any case, then you are in danger of becoming hateful, resentful and vindictive because no one will right away know how to value your communal contribution. You will feel ever so rejected, but all the same you will know, especially now that I have reminded you, that 'what it's all about' is your increasing recognition of folk-characteristics and your acknowledgement of your folk-nature – which is an aspect of, and an introduction to, your human nature. Because here's the rub: You are being introduced to your sound human nature, which you may have heard of, and you may even have imagined that you know all about it, conceptually, religiously, but not until now have you made that physical contact tantamount to true and beautiful faith.

The fact that human evolution introduces itself physically rather than on one or the other side of the developmental spectrum – I mean on the side of mind or the side of body, intellect or will, nature or nurture and so on – also implies the various truly physical reactions, which, of course, are bound to stump all the modern developmental sciences, especially the hundred and one biologies, which know nothing of the whole human being as such and especially nothing of communal men, women and children who struggle with the transition from development to evolution. As a consequence the various unique opportunities for actual wellbeing are mistaken for diminishments of health, treated accordingly, and then failures are written off.

It all begins, what we are concerned with in this essay, with an invitation to evolve. This is something that comes upon a human being when the time for it is ripe. It amounts to a specific spiritual experience. One is overwhelmed and one reacts. Since one is overwhelmed, one is not aware that one is reacting. What it takes is someone who will respond to our reactive behaviour. Such a response will then allow us to respond in turn and what we have then is <u>human-natural affection</u>. No further reaction is now possible.

Our <u>folk-nature is human-naturally affectionate</u>. We make no excuses for that. We only know that, at the end of the line, this is the way to be. This is the way to be finally. I am not saying that action arises out of this. The way we behave, act and suffer is a separate matter and does not interfere with the way we are now. Nonetheless human-naturally affectionate being is expressive, demonstrative and exemplary. It is a comfortable way to be and it comforts.

Can we continue to be human-naturally affectionate? We can, if we go among those who are not human-naturally affectionate. This, I suppose, is what one would expect, because good spirit itself is among us in order to be among more of us. And certainly there are those whose human nature is a folk-nature. That is the way to be for them, and all their doing centres on this.[1] They may be a comfort to many and they may even encourage others to be as they are and to teach them how to stop making themselves uncomfortable. However they cannot make them evolve, because this is a gift of god and only merciful good spirit knows where to place that gift.

*

Those whose evolution has begun, will soon enough know how far they are to evolve, i.e. to the point of folk-nature, or to where they act out the truth and become creative on behalf of others. Many are picked but few are chosen. Those who are chosen can certainly help those who are picked identify, as soon as possible, all the folk-characteristics that are masked by diverse reactions to them. It helps to keep in mind that in our reaction is foreshadowed that to which we react, as our reactions stem from our individual will, which takes on the very

---

[1] Just today I heard of the 'Gesundheit Institute'. Patch Adams, MD, would certainly fit this description.

shape of what we fear – that which we would do well to welcome. And here we have within us, if we believe this, the one who first demonstrated this major ethical strategy in his own life. Those who are to have the wisdom of their folk-nature also have access to this priceless folk-memory, as they fully accept, within themselves and in their being, his guiding presence. They say 'lead, kindly light' and are able to navigate their way through all the obstructions of modern culture and civilization without resisting or taking umbrage.

*

<u>Modern culture and civilization</u>, by definition, obstruct the evolution of human beings. A thing-culture and a thing-civilization is not truly creative but rather it is productive. What is more, it is thing-productive, in anxious reaction to that particular growth-stimulus which is evolutionary in nature. Such a reaction is perfectly understandable. Once we are hardened in our various developmental formulas, which arise, as we mentioned earlier in this essay, out of a misunderstanding of development as 'the end of the line' for human beings, we are not going to take kindly to evolutionary growth, because it does at first seem to take the initiative out of our often all too proud and productive hands. While the true end of development could be called the distinction of spirit and flesh, which distinction is to facilitate evolution, all the many efforts that are made somehow to incorporate separate spirit (the so-called 'pure' religions, for example) and to vitalize separate flesh (particle physics for example) merely protract the agony of modern man, who refuses to suffer his anxiety. Instead he invests more and more raw energy in his various futile attempts at a one-sided, developmental culmination. Evolution, however, begins with the marriage of spirit and flesh.

*

13

Evolution also begins with the killer instinct.

What I described earlier as <u>uncomfortable, inconvenient and disagreeable</u>, all three at once, reactionary forces that announce the onset of folk nature, turns, upon closer inspection, into the primal-instinctive reaction of the human being to <u>psyche, ego and identity</u>, all three as one. The simple truth of the matter, before going into detail, teaches us here that the impulse to kill another human being is the sign, and the only sign we have if we want to depend on a sign and to wait for it before we respond – of the onset of human-natural evolution.

Let him in whom this great hatred surfaces understand as soon as possible what is going on. The hatred arises within him and within himself lives both knowledge and understanding of evolution plus the readiness for it.

But oh dear, that is saying a lot! Instead of knowledge and understanding I should perhaps say: the ability to know and understand plus a degree of <u>guilt and shame</u> to the extent that he has not yet acquainted himself with the eventuality of his evolution. And instead of 'readiness' I should perhaps say: 'the need for readiness', or 'the right time' for evolution. On one hand the '<u>son of man</u>'[1] must come when we are not looking but on the other hand he would not come unless we had developed at least to the point of readiness and that therefore we 'should' be able to come up with the appropriate response. If instead we cling to the <u>guilt, the shame and the resentment</u> and respond to that, in other words to our own reaction, in terms of <u>revenge, criticism and blame</u>, then we miss out on the evolution and

---

[1] I feel free to introduce this concept, 'the son of man', from the Christian Gospels, because these are the first documents we have that deal with the reality and the beginning of human evolution. As usual, I try to make it my main business to translate from modern into contemporary.

have to wait for the next time when the killer-instinct surfaces, if it does.

In the meantime, of course, we can do a great deal, in terms of repentance and truth-education, to re-establish ourselves on the development-ladder.

The truth-education will primarily urge us in the direction of: What exactly is it worth to me that I vent my anger instead of being a bit more forgiving and merciful? When have I gained anything more substantial than a bit of gloating, a momentary appearance of triumph in case anyone should be watching, since the upper hand, whenever I have kept it for a spell, shortly cramps and I become incapable of holding a decent argument, with emphasis on honest right rather than self-image.

*

There is never so great a gap between the incarnate spirit and the conscious human vessel as at that moment when god says: Now let humanity be your guide. Not humanism but humanity, the essence of being. That moment is the so-called Day of the Lord, capitalized and projected, fearfully, whimsically, theologically, all three as one, into the unknowable future, even though the very next moment was ready for all who should choose, almost two-thousand years ago. This is the Day of Judgment, when the last stone is fitted into place and here is your house, your home, your mansion. What, you don't fancy it? You consider yourself not quite ready? You would rather do the decent thing, be kind, cling to your mother's apron strings? Mother Church? Mother Country? Someone will end up being sacrificed, you understand that, don't you? Your own child perhaps, because the wind blows wrong? A hundred-thousand soldiers because clearly that country is your enemy? Your brother who disputes your rights? That should put it off for a while. There are so many issues that still need to be settled – the burial of your father for but one example – before you have the time to accept even the comfort of your folk-nature, not to mention the ethical dimension of eternal life on earth. The killer-instinct will allow you in the meantime to see to any and every eventuality.

Not all commit themselves to the over-up in the modern half-way house, existing either to the left or to the right. What a blessing it is, to come across a man who has made his decision and dropped out of the rat-race only to find, that much he could only partly achieve takes care of itself completely. What a treat to come across a woman who has made her peace with her female nature and she leaves all the latest cultural calamities to the newspapers. They bring up their children, these two and they feel they know how to do it, no worries, the parental love in their brain, blood and groin combined will solve the problems. In the meanwhile, smiling betimes, they put up with what has to be put up with; it makes them stronger.

Should we ask them, do they believe in God?

This is not something we think about, they say. Are we not all aware of how much we were born with and how much we depend on the good will of those around us? There was a time when we imagined we were responsible for everything that happened to us and unless we planned and controlled every inch of our day and every move we made we would end up in trouble and pain. Then someone, one day, who was passing through here, a traveller from who knows where, told us he knew he was well taken care of and the way he said it made us sit up and take notice. Was it what he said or maybe the way he said it? Surely both. In any case, we were able to relax then. We have lived in this house for nearly forty years now, our children and grandchildren help us when we need help. And our door is always open to strangers, like yourself. Are you ready for a bite to eat now?

*

I was nineteen years old at the time and not content. My studies at university were not going well, nothing seemed to lift me out of indifference to whatever approached. A friend and his young wife had invited me to stay with them for a week. They were genuinely kind to me, although I could not have been a pleasant person for them to have around.

I had got into the habit of helping myself out a little by writing occasional verses and one evening I went for a stroll in the neighbourhood. This was in Toronto, in late autumn and it was cool enough to enjoy the benefit of a scarf and a cap on my head. Not much light was left as I sat down on a park bench, with the intention of jotting down a few lines in a diary I had brought along.

When I raised m eyes I saw an elderly couple who had stopped to look at me from where the path took a turn in the direction of a few houses I hadn't really been aware of until then. Two slightly stooped eighty-year-olds, I reckoned, and they were smiling. I said hello and to my surprise they came over to talk to me. They were poorly dressed but clean, a carefully mended appearance, I recall. Mind you, this happened sixty years ago, so what I remember best is that the woman asked: 'Are you cold?' I said: 'A little,' and they came closer. Then the man said: 'Are you hungry?'

Well, I was a little, so I said yes, but I had no idea why they wanted to know. Then they invited me to come along to their house where they would make me a cup of coffee. I understood that they cared about me in a way I did not readily recognize and this intrigued me, so I followed them, for maybe a hundred

17

yards, to where they lived. I believe their house was one of several in a terrace. We made our way in through a badly painted front door. They moved slowly, almost as if they were doing everything for the first time and as if at any moment some happy innovation might surprise them. I wish I could describe more accurately the effect the old furniture had on me, the scuffed lino on the floor, the chequered plastic table cloth and the old sink with the single tap for cold water.

'Sit here,' the woman said. She motioned me to a chair by the table. 'This is Dan,' she said, pointing to the man, who was hanging up his coat 'and I'm Rose. Now you'll soon be warm.'

I don't think I said my name. It didn't seem important. After a while a cup of coffee appeared and an assortment of biscuits. Then I was offered a sandwich and was glad of it. I recall I was in a strange mood. Baucis and Philemon, I thought. I existed in a story, not in reality. I observed, but I also felt strangely complete for a change and no demands were being made on me.

I cannot recall the ensuing conversation, indeed if there was any, but to this day the way I felt, how I was, remains clearly in my memory. I should have asked them, surely, about themselves, about their past life but I didn't. I only sat and was catered to; did I want more coffee, another sandwich, all to do with the present moment. The strangeness of the situation did not enter my mind until some time afterwards, after I had jotted down several verses, recalling the incident in a realistic light. 'Dan and Rose' I called my poem and I sent it to a publisher. That seemed like the appropriate thing to do right away at the time.

It was one of my early experiences of what I now call folk-nature in this essay. In the meantime I have had ample opportunity to compare this implicit trust and simple, almost child-like care for another person to what I mean by moral and fully

18

ethical attitudes and behaviour and I have decided that it deserves another look but on its own terms.

I have a grandson who appeals to this folk-nature in myself. He is still a teenager and prone to passing hasty judgment but his nature is inwardly informed of the connectedness of all that is. At times he comes out with statements one would only expect from an adult made wise by much experience. What I seem to see in him is a present soul, to the influence of which on himself he does not react. This is perhaps the central characteristic of a folk-nature. Those of us who naturally develop are always to a degree at risk in a modern environment and out of our willingness to rise to the occasion of that risk, our creativity becomes productive (we become creative) and we make our contribution to our community. I would not be surprised if my grandson never made or produced anything but that his value would always lie in his presence among us. He makes no demands on anyone. Even as a child he seemed remarkably possessed of a loveable, self-contained spirit. He was sent to a primary school for a few weeks and the inappropriateness, for him, of such a system right away became laughably obvious.

My main reason for drawing attention to this folk-nature as to a special case alongside human development is the misunderstanding that can cause harm to such human beings who should be valued mainly for who they are, because that alone allows us to draw on the advantages of their presence among us.

So for example we notice that anyone who passes negative judgment on my grandson soon feels the pain of his mistake. Criticism makes next to no impression. Neglect, rejection are felt but not resented by him. In fact resentment of any kind seems to be impossible for him, which is why those of us who quickly resent feel duly shamed at times.

*

This draws our own attention to whether or not we have a soul. Perhaps it may be put as simply as that. The folk-nature of someone draws attention to itself inasmuch as it inadvertently informs us of our reaction to our soul and very likely also to our ongoing modern confirmation of that reaction. Such reaction may have become intentional and habitual in us, while here right beside us someone exists who has no need to react in this manner. How is that possible? we ask. How can he blithely take in stride, without thinking, what for us has become such an issue? In fact this has become almost the central issue of our modern existence, namely that we see ample reason for bolstering our psychic knowledge, because it promises to deal with what we experience as a potentially overwhelming threat and danger – and yet it will not solve the problem outright. Mercifully it will not put paid to the lingering horror of the strangeness that interferes with our ambition to find peace by amalgamating, accumulating and coagulating. No matter how many Soviet Unions or European Unions or African Unions we come up with, dissolution stares us in the face, the more nastily the more we cling.

What good is psyche if soul is required?

Granted, our works may begin with our willingness to overcome our reaction to soul, our resistance and rejection of soul – of god, let us say right away, since a soul is the true god's presence within us. And we feel we ought to produce works, that much is clear – except, it seems, for those who do not reject god within them, even to begin with, so there they are. They seem perfectly content not producing works. Their soul rests within them, for purpose of example. We have the choice, either to love them or to reject them too, along with our soul – though our rejection of our soul is made to appear downright absurd now and perhaps we feel urged to reconsider, in which case god is justified in sending us these reminders. These catalytic transition-phenomena!

They remind us of our unnatural rebellion – unnatural once we intend the accident. We contemplate that which could not be helped, i.e. the momentary denial of god, (of the son of man who must come when we do not expect!) and we turn it into conscious practice and intentional performance. I mean those of us who do that, of course, and not those who have come to the realization that our bad behaviour had for a time become habitual inasmuch as we mistook our psyche for something worth a second look.

Surely we cannot expect those who do not know the joy of doing the work that is theirs to do, to take kindly to those who are not yet creatively active. Those who pay grudging lip service to their instinct for self-preservation, in the sweat of their brow or pretentiously, insist we should all do the same and they take umbrage at the creative ethic from start to finish. They resent the folk-nature, however it makes its appearance. I suspect that betimes they indulge in a little ethnic cleansing, to support the bogus justice of their unimaginative existence all the more thoroughly. Can they be forced by law or by social opprobrium to place soul-cooperation ahead of self-preservation? Not very likely, I should think.

* *

After browsing again, recently, in Thomas Mann's reworking of the Joseph story, I could not help but wonder, was there finally all that much of a discrepancy between this author's take on that story and the original one, if indeed one can with justice speak of an original, where so many mythic tributaries flow into an underground, folk-collective stream? Or does it matter all that much, because surely what counts is not historic accuracy but contemporary usefulness? And Thomas Mann does, in my opinion, depict this Joseph as possessed truly, and at first tragically, of a folk-nature. Neither the child nor the man if portrayed as showing signs of having to do inward battle for the possession of his soul (like Jacob, his father). He is depicted as someone who waits for his problems to sort themselves out and who enjoys observing how good fortune falls into his lap. All he has to do, really, is take note of the spiritual clues. The author identifies him cryptically as "blessed both from above and from below". The ethical environs of an Abraham, Isaac and Jacob was not ready for such a one. A much older civilization could understand him and employ him usefully, as the late-cultural pharaoh of Egypt did. Ultimately – and coincidentally – his own vastly extended family owed him their very survival – on account of yet another of Joseph's dreams.

Mann makes a meal, a delicious meal, we might say, of the discrepancy between wit and muscle, between imagination and the daily grind. The title of Mann's book, 'Joseph and his Brothers', says it all, really. Soul and psyche. Cooperation and force – and yet not quite, because this epic novel is still a modern creation, much attached to windy mythologizing and the bluff of magic. It takes a thoroughly contemporary mind to appreciate the evolutionary folk-nature, as I mean it here, in comparison to the more creative, evolutionary human nature. Thomas Mann could hardly be blamed for leaving the very thought of 'the folk' – das Volk – as such, to one side after what his compatriots had meant by it. So the characterization of the folk-nature rightly falls to us then, for we might say that we have the holocaust of two world wars behind us and that we recognize the proximity of a contemporary reality even as tragic modernity fades.

*

There are two reasons why I use the word 'folk' to describe the nature and characteristics of those who demonstrate this particular side of humanity which seems to me, in our present day, especially worth of recognition and needful of acknowledgment.

First, what I associate with 'folk' is the incalculable beginning, simply in 'years gone by', of a <u>spirit</u> that has always revealed itself, and still does so in our day, as perfectly imaginable and therefore immune to <u>criticism</u>. (By the way, whatever is perfectly imaginable stands on its own feet and, strange to say, the wind of change blows right through it.) I myself happen to know this <u>folk-spirit</u> first hand and it has taken me some time to appreciate the quantity of it. By its quantity I mean the sheer weight of it in terms of character-influence. I have been more interested in personality because it, as a concept, allows me to speak for human beings both in general and in the particular. By honouring the person, one includes, by implication, the folk-spirit without actually naming it and one refers to what I have called the weight of it in terms of 'all flesh', as blessed, in contrast to carnality, as wild, or unblessed. Folk-spirit endows us with character and allows me to speak of all beings other than human beings as endowed with characteristics. Both character and characteristics are totally imaginable and therefore immune to criticism. We know the folk-spirit directly as character and indirectly as characteristics.

My 'characterization' of this folk-spirit of course allows me to understand its suitability – allows us to 'see' how and why it lends itself so readily – to myth, legend and story. The time-honoured formula "once upon a time" is the favourite and most suitable introduction – both to it and of it. All we have to do is say something imaginary like: "There once was a man who could speak only in words of a single syllable," or even: "Far back in the 'seventies', before they had built any Public Offices at Simla,..."[1] and we feel the folk-spirit settling into us, hopeful of favourable reception. Tales, stories, fables, sagas – all that is narrative, vocally or literally, with the purpose of outfitting us with capacities and abilities for facing the world honourably – this is the gift – we might say 'in the gift' – of the folk-spirit as it has helped us navigate our passage through the centuries. The essence of it is make-belief, and the purpose of it is always make-believe – to make us believe – namely this and that which in terms of imagination is totally trustworthy.

Shall we speculate now how long and arduous is the path from honourable make-belief to true, fundamental and initiative faith?

*

Then there is the voice with which the folk-spirit speaks, which is properly the <u>vernacular</u>. You will not find any but the most ordinary, every-day language spoken or written by those whose work is inspired by it. It is not the language that recreates itself, out of itself, in order to foster renewal, for the folk-spirit seeks merely to render the true human being self-reliant and possessed of confidence. I mention Thomas Mann, the German author again, who in the book 'Joseph and his Brothers' celebrates, in the most non-vernacular, artistic language, the folk-characteristics of Joseph, the elder son of Isaac and Rachel. Joseph the dreamer, who is cast into a well and subsequently raised to the side of Pharaoh's caretaker; who is cast into prison, only to be raised even higher, to become the Steward of the kingdom in the name of Pharaoh.

The children of the folk-spirit are taken care of, one does not worry about them. Of course they are not all exceptional. Most are barely noticed by those who peruse the world with a public

---

[1] From: 'The Other Man' – 'Plain Tales of the Hills', by R. Kipling.

eye. Nonetheless their influence, as bearers of the folk-spirit, is crucial in terms of solidarity and preservation of human community.

Which also explains why they add nothing to Society. They stand at the edge of Society and when they bother to look in, they smile. They do not themselves develop or evolve but are products of evolution.

*

We might also draw the comparison – if not the contrast – between 'folk' and '<u>people</u>'.

I have always used the word 'people' to point to the carriers of the popular spirit, which is one from the dark range and not at all given to promote growth. In fact both development and especially evolution are anathema to it, mostly because <u>resurrection</u> permeates all human growth, while <u>popularity</u>, as we know, insists, commonly with a vengeance, on states and standards that are to safeguard the <u>status quo</u>. So we can speak of a human being with folk characteristics, but people, if pressed, would always insist on their righteousness, because they presume they have a right to it. Hence they illustrate plentifully that we are not damned for what we do but for what we neglect to do and refrain from doing for no good reason. People play it safe, take care not to step over the line; you might say they broaden their outlook by limiting their expenses. By comparison, it is the folk-nature of a human being that 'short-circuits', as it were, all tendencies to idolatry, superstition, idealism, and also to any supernatural leanings that might have been inherited; on account of the folk-spirit these do not even have to be faced for us to be rid of them.

*

25

What the word '<u>folk</u>' finally suggests is a ready communality that is downright instinctive, wherefore it operates not on a level of consciousness but quite simply in line with daily usage. In those where this folk-spirit demands strong self-expression, we come across the most pronounced emphasis on fairness, justice and equality of moral consideration – apparently in the total absence of self-interest. What it amounts to however is the characteristic expression of an instinctive 'feel' for communality, which implies, with no need for special mention, that whatever is good for you is bound to be good for me too.

This 'feel' for communality, I man in comparison to concrete understanding, allows us correctly to assess a situation as it were in the dark. And if something does not 'feel' right, I mean something someone has said or something that has been done, we do not criticize. This, I believe, I have mentioned before, that criticism, the spirit of criticism itself, cannot achieve a foothold in any folk-nature. At the same time then, as one would expect, one must not demand a useful critique from us – (I make common cause with the common folk here). No, in the face of anything disingenuous we feel ill at ease, we step back and simply say no. Honesty, uprightness, integrity of character must be allowed to win out, so we strongly feel and those who cut corners and disrespect what we mean by decency of conduct and behaviour simply do not get our support.

*

The single most hated enemy of the folk-spirit is <u>universalism</u>, whether in thought or in performance. And as is always the case, we call those our enemies who incorporate our weaknesses, our leanings, I mean, to our own disadvantage.

By universalism I mean a tendency to thought and action that dispenses with diversity and degree. Simply put, universalist is the notion that the universe somewhere comes to an end

26

so that we can rest assured of not being disturbed. So on one hand we have the opinion that everything is either black or white, good or bad, and on the other hand we do not allow for the singularity of a being to find its place in the sun.

The main universalist theory is that we should tie all our principles to one theory and call it truth; also that there must be a common denominator for 'everything'. Reality, in other words, needs to be 'boiled down' for the universalist, so that he might have it in his grasp. The folk-spirit works in the opposite direction. It tends to display the infinite multiplicity and variety of what is real and would go out of its sway to point us in that direction. By 'going out of its way' I mean that it allows us to become naturally confused and even persuades us intentionally to bring down confusion on our heads in order to persuade us to escape from the danger of the universalist straitjacket.[1]

The folk-spirit, not being critical, supplies right away the cure too, in terms of folk-nature, so if we learn to appreciate this spirit, we do not have to knock ourselves out, by drink, smoke and drugs for example, in order to escape from the evils of the planned Society or from the traps and snares of our various simpleton-philosophies based on the lust for insane control. The trick is to discover within ourselves that singular, initiative love of truth that painlessly cuts through whatever resistance we have allowed – or even encouraged – to accumulate and to blend into our human being as magical structures upon which we are liable to rely in pursuit of our adult immaturity.

Folk-spirit and folk-nature – both benevolent opposition to the universalist fallacy. So we might ask: What is the main point when we contemplate discernment of spirits? After all

---

[1] The poet Arthur Rimbaud comes to mind and his 'dérèglement de tous les sens'.

god is one, is merciful good spirit. We however present a great banquet of humanity. We are not only all different, all unique, as we like to remind one another at a time when the trivializing superficiality sown by the dead and by the reluctantly still half-alive sprouts all over the earth as the one universalist wet blanket of weeds – but we are approached by good spirit in a number of ways and then we, of course, initially react to those ways, because our shortcomings are highlighted by them. Those of us who quickly (or at last) identify and take the responsibility for those reactions sometimes have to fight our corner against those who do not do that, but they blame the person next to them, the government and God Almightily. They do <u>that</u> with spirit too, but of course this is bad spirit, as which it may be identified by those who know and possibly even love good spirit – in any one of its (his) guises).

The folk-spirit is such a guise specifically in favour of those who long for community but can only come up with communism. In this present, sufficiently rational sense, a communist is someone who by hook or by crook, but sadly not by self-discipline, aims at community, hopes for at least communality but ends in the universalism of any number of massive states, which do then have to be 'kept in line', i.e. governed, from the outside. Massive states are what we 'fall into' if we are not careful. It amounts to the same whether we fall in love, in charity or in altruism; it happens, and if we do not take care it ends in a psychic state, which is massive and not integral. Subsequently the lack of all supportive integrity is highlighted by 'breakup'.

Where merciful good spirit is not accepted as such – and a strong constitution is required for that – it goes elsewhere and appeals in a guise, such as folk-spirit, or the spirit of community, for example. We do well to inform ourselves of such as this. And if we can make sense of it, we do equally well to say so.

*

Characterization, as we have learned, is the main tool of the folk-spirit. We may know it by that. It allows us to understand what otherwise would only puzzle us. So, for example, communism, as I mean it here, can spread like an epidemic plague and we come upon the most detailed descriptions of it in the sympathetic works of Dostoyevsky for example and Chekhov points it out to us in many of his compassionate tales.[1] Such literature is bound to move a few souls in the direction of self-discipline. For the great mass of people however the corrective limit always has to come from outside, and so we may observe repressive universalist forms in action in the hands of demonic individuals. This then is what people call communism, when in fact it is that which limits communism and eventually stamps it out, as events show.

So let us not confuse the fatal powers that bring pressure to bear, with that which, if it were to continue to spread, it would devastate the earth and humanity would be forgotten.

Communism, to repeat, is the psychic state or condition brought on by universalist thinking and feeling (universalist malingering) which, if it continues long enough, is eventually repressed by demonic forces, from outside, wherever self-discipline has not caught on. Those who cannot be bothered with inward home-making and housekeeping are then plagued, after a short period of psychic high spirits, and their condition worsens, to be addressed eventually by accident, misfortune and forceful 'conditioning', which people label as communism.

---

[1] Or in his play: 'Three Sisters' – "Oh Moscow, Moscow!" etc.

If we suppose now that it gets us anywhere to castigate the fatal corrective, we are mistaken. There are as many kinds of communism as there are ethnic divergences from the universalist norm. For those who can accept it, liberalism is only the soft underbelly of the communism plague, due to its own lack of self-realization.

So what is popularly called communism and liberalism is in fact the fatal corrective of those two plagues and should instead, perhaps, be called something like divine judgment – in essence good spirit's merciful safeguarding of humanity for the earth and of the earth for human beings.

We do not call it drug abuse when we take some poor semi-conscious individual, who has swallowed a handful of amphetamines, to the cold shower. We do not call it inebriation when we poor coffee into the actor who has got himself into a drunken state and he is due on stage. We might call it tough love, and we will keep at the chap even though he tries to fight us off. Perhaps he will thank us afterwards.

Will we thank god eventually for his tough love when everything else failed – for curing us of liberalism and communism and similar 'stimulants'? Only if we come to our senses. Only if we embrace the true folk-spirit and allow ourselves to be educated. A tough call sometimes, to be sure, in the company of those who know only black and white and lack the imagination for diversity and degree.

*

The 'initiative love of truth' I have mentioned is both something that occurs to us and something we can adopt. It is initiated in us and we can initiate it in others. It is the classic calling-card of the folk-spirit in our folk-nature, where we may identify it and then carry it out.

Recognizing it as the impulse that it is, is not the easiest thing in the world for everybody. As a thing it is nothing more than a disturbance in our routine. Generally we resent such disturbances because our independent will is challenged. So shunning the call of truth is interpreted and praised as persistence. We should not be expected to suffer all the interruptions of our plans gladly. But here is what matters now. The truth only <u>seems</u> to interrupt us, when in fact it only needs to be noticed, to be taken account of and not to be brushed aside. I wonder why this is so difficult for so many of us. I expect it has to do with the 'bloody tenacity' with which we go about our business sometimes. That would be one reason. We get so wrapped up in the 'what' and the 'how' that the 'why' refuses to enter our heads. "Why are you doing that?" someone asks us and we hate him. We want to be liberated from the consciousness of our imperfections, from the nagging doubts that assail us as soon as we begin to reflect; mechanical labours, performed in haste, stupefy us to an extent. The thoughtless routine of the sleepwalker attracts us too. Consciousness, self- or other-, is liable to turn into a searing flame unless we shut it out. We are asleep in the house, we hear violent knocking at the door, we open the door and look at a wall of fire, approaching fast. We grab our car keys and speed off. Next day we return and nothing, but nothing is left.

It does not have to come to that. However we are and whatever we do, we can remain open to interruption by initiative truth, whether from within or from without. In either case we will sense it naturally. By 'naturally' I mean folk-naturally, during the course of our daily routine, however we are just behaving ourselves – when we least expect it the initiative truth interrupts us, yes of course, naturally, that has to be said; so in some fashion that surprises, though not necessarily all that unpleasant every time. Let the emphasis be on the total attention we pay right away – even while we continue with what we are doing.

Does that sound contradictory? Well, of course it does, and it is to an extent. However the extent depends on us. Like everything we do, the more we do it the better we get at it. I am 'speaking' to those whose folk-nature has begun to draw attention to itself, not in terms of growth, of development and evolution, but simply as <u>the singular focus of their casual existence</u>. Here, we say, is something worth keeping in mind. It seems to work like an accompaniment. 'Let it be my secret. Yes, my secret. Come to think of it, it would seem wrong somehow to talk about it. And oh, if someone preached it at me, I would deny all knowledge.'

So we make a point of 'letting our little light shine' even though at first it almost blinded us – or confused us like a will-o'-the-wisp when we still imagined we might stare at it and settle down with it.

No, the <u>initiative truth</u>, once we no longer shy away from it as from some pointless interruption, becomes our faithful companion. Initially we know it as nature and spirit entwined and we cannot right away see the need for any difference. Eventually however we catch on to the beauty of either allowing ourselves to be initiated <u>or</u> to initiate. The two as one occur to us as a rather wonderful arrangement. We take kindly now to being initiated from within, even though it seems to hurt a bit at times as our resistance is overcome, and we rather look forward to being able to initiate outwardly, in one way or another, for one or another reason; it always gives us a renewed sense of purpose. And if it should be our appointed task to shape world affairs, nothing succeeds so promptly as our cooperation with folk-spirit – which is hardly surprising, since the <u>folk-spirit is the special interest merciful good spirit takes in our everyday welfare.</u>

*

The truth I may initiate is of the sort that allows people to get on with what they are doing without taking notice, while folk do take notice. They take notice in spite of themselves. The fact that I have a handle, as it were, on initiative truth is obvious to folk but totally irrelevant to people. The worst that can happen is that my initiative truth is ignored and then I know where I stand and no need for regret – except, of course, that folk-company would have been a pleasure. Folk are especially good company. They are not cultured and they are not civilized. By which I do not mean to say that folk are 'uncivilized boors'. It seems the time has come to say a word about Culture and Civilization. (I capitalize idols.)

*

In the end it is amazing what all we get away with, if we are not careful, in the name of Culture and Civilization. I would like to identify Culture, for our present purpose, as the sumtotal of all the efforts people nowadays make to appease the demons of popularity. Culture as an idol is, of course, something quite different from culture as the basket into which we throw all the 'Art' that has been manufactured or is being manufactured. The demons of popularity demand that we become soulless consumers of pointless commodities and that we focus on this to keep us interested in continuing to survive and to hell with life – with the emphasis on 'to hell with life'. Life from the popular point of view amounts to a huge threat because its emphasis is on truth and growth. The demons of popularity are 'cast out', if I may use that expression, by any attention we pay to the truth and by any interest we take in growth; in human development and evolution.

In this essay we limit ourselves to folk, which is to say: to human beings who value the truth specifically in the sense of initiative, while growth it automatic. We have already seen that

the initiative truth 'bounces off' people, so that any demon appeasement in the vicinity leaves the folk-nature cold and the
folk-spirit turns away. In the meantime people have to let those
demons know that they are on their side, and willing to shun
life, i.e. growth and the truth. That keeps the demons at bay on
a regular basis. All the same a lot of effort has to go into the
rejection of truth and much energy needs to be invested in
making sure that growth remains massive, such as the growth
of the economy, the growth of national and personal prestige,
the increase of health and happiness, of sensual pleasure, the
expansion of ego and so on, which is all outside- and inside-
growth, i.e. mere accumulation, and not really human growth at
all, which is inward and outward.

*

What I mean by <u>Civilization</u> is gradual conflict external to
human being and behaviour that keeps people occupied with
popular issues, which is to say with such issues as arise from
self-centred preoccupation with 'popular demons'[1]. Survival of
the ego or self is eventually turned into survival of the globe,
once the survival of 'the Nation' no longer seems feasible.

A civilized individual can be depended on not to disrupt the
general status quo until his own particular status quo is threatened by that of another, whereupon he is liable to arrive at
some cynical decision in terms of self-preservation with disrespect to the status quo of other people. The civilized nations of
Europe only reflect, as nations generally do, the overwhelming
collectivity of individual people. We suppose we have made a
discovery when we suddenly realize that 'the destruction of
civilization' is a real danger, until we are reminded how much

---

[1] A demon is a spirit that is bad inasmuch as we merge with it or are possessed by it rather than using it as an invitation to be truly creative. Examples are materialism, spiritualism, egotism etc. etc.

of such a danger was sensed prior to the second world war, during the Thirty Years War or in India when Alexander knocked at the gate.

Fear for the status quo is a popular demon that looks for appeasement in terms of efforts at reform, of attempts to change the world, in short by my will to change your will or by your intellect to influence my intellect. If you decide you want to change my will, you must have some notion of it being a threat to yours. Certainly if you wanted to do me some real good, you would set me an example of it and leave me at liberty to adopt it or not. The same goes for any intellectual persuasion of which you would like me to have the benefit. The civilizing influence does not set examples but it propagates conflict, always in the hope of achieving an end state in which the civilizing agent will at last be left alone – 'to decay in peace and comfort', a human being will say, because he knows what is going on.

Human beings, for example, do not create art-works in order to glory in their individual talent and genius but so as to set good examples that will coincidentally protect them against Culture and Civilization. At the same time human development is a growth process. What is involved is learning and practice, inward progress in the presence of outside happenings and often even in response to external dangers. When people come along and laud these human emergency measures as popular achievements and pay piles of this or that currency for being able to hang a Da Vincy painting of Christ in their private retreat – well, among them be it, as folk around where I live might say. I speak of art-works as emergency measures because they are what a human being does as he emerges from one stage of development to the next. I also distinguish between art-workers and artists. The latter participate to some extent, sadly often by choice, in the conflict that is Civilization and in the appeasement of popular demons that is Culture.

So by Civilization I mean every effort to prolong conflict, such as between pessimists and optimists, between humanists and materialists, between peaceniks and war-mongers, between nation and nation and finally between any one status quo and another. The only real differences that comes to light is the one between the status quo of people who do not cope with their energy and the status quo of those who fear for their.

As for Culture as appeasement of popular demons – for our own understanding, any attempt to name these demons is pointless because they are legion.

*

Folk are neither cultured nor civilized. This has come up especially now when we take an interest specifically in human beings who do not develop but are born intact and therefore ready for evolution. As a consequence, the popular demons make no impression on them but they do inadvertently keep reminding them of who they are and where they should go – and where not to go – for their livelihood.

Our folk-nature does, after all, encourage us to grow up. We are not allowed to rest content with our inborn faculties unexercised or with our inborn tastes and tempers unchallenged. So although we gravitate towards companionship, we are never quite able to ignore our own <u>personal limitations</u> against which we invariably chafe until we make sense of them and incorporate them. So for example the <u>limitation in contact with the other sex</u>, which may initially be experienced as a shortcoming because we do not seem to be able to identify our male or female nature, are incorporated, in that we become masculine or feminine in honour of the other gender. Where this sense of honour has been lost, we pile up problems for ourselves until we find it again.

Then, of course, there is the <u>limitation of our individuality</u> vis-à-vis anyone else's individuality. So far as our folk-nature is concerned, we are more likely than not to ignore that difference and simply to fall in with 'how someone else is constituted' – and in that way we are liable to 'sell ourselves short'. Our <u>constitution</u> however is not what we bring forward from our birthright as human beings but rather how we are and how we have become due to our make-up – which is the result of our interaction with our conditions and surroundings.

This interaction, more or less liberally with beings and things, leaves within us a <u>deposit</u> of sorts to which we have <u>no direct access</u> and for which we <u>cannot be readily responsible</u>, however it is more than liable to influence our behaviour. It occurs, this deposit, to the degree that during our casual interaction with beings and things we have had intercourse with <u>critical spirit</u>. [1]

So on one hand we have our <u>folk-soul</u>, merciful good spirit within us upon which we may lean and with which (or whom) we may choose to interrelate. Depending on how we were brought up, we are more or less familiar with our soul and able to take advantage of the fact that we are endowed with one.

On the other hand, we bear within us something that has no relation to our soul and it is not even soul-like (psychic) but rather an accidental indication of how, until now, we have coped with critical spirit, with our reactions and responses to critical spirit and crucially it is an indication (initially for others and not for ourselves) of our actual cooperation with critical spirit, which may have has tragic consequences.

*

---

[1] It is mostly up to us whether we experience 'it' as a being or a thing..

37

The upshot of what I have so far only referred to as a deposit within us (not in us or inside us, by the way, but within us, n.b.) is the separation of personality from individuality, with which all human beings, since the beginning of the modern era (these recent two millennia), are germinally born.[1]

We are grateful for this separation because it makes possible our freedom or salvation for us as mature human beings. It makes it possible but cannot guarantee it, because our faithful cooperation with good spirit, our love of truth and practice of unconditional love, etc. is required from us. In the absence of our creative input, (whether overtly or covertly) as based on this fortuitous separation, critical spirit tends to move in, as criticism, and to make its mark – to leave its evidence – its deposit of malignity. This <u>malignance,</u> that is due to our compliance with critical spirit, tends to vitiate the 'marriage' of individuality and personality that implies our freedom and for which we choose to hold ourselves responsible as evolving human beings.

*

Human beings who have developed and begun to evolve – in other words whose resurrection is underway, are aware of this deposit of critical spirit and of the perverse hold it can have on them and they know it as something to be <u>creatively overcome</u> and now and again simply to be negated. It is therefore specifically for those among us whose folk-nature draws attention to itself while folk-spirit empowers them, to learn to recognize this critical handicap, which I have described as a malignant deposit within, and <u>to repress it</u>, or rather to <u>press past it</u> into the <u>reality which exists as good spirit and chaste flesh as one.</u>

---

[1] I would ask the reader to keep in mind that I write not for those who are perfect and good but for human beings who have been influenced, like myself, by the modern mind-set and are inhibited by modern prejudices.

Any critical deposit therefore inadvertently[1] indicates to the wide-awake owner of folk-humanity the available true reality into which he may press.

*

Prior to the division of massive ancient being into individuality and personality,[2] when no such thing as what modern man means by personality and by individuality yet existed and when these problematic entities, riven by criticism, could only perhaps have been predicted by prophetic narrative, ancient man thought and behaved differently. The event of personality and individuality as such coming separately into being, this right away implied the liberation of ancient man from his massive existence in which darkness and light unpredictably intermingled. One imagines that the advent of something like a happy integration of massive existence must have been anticipated, desired, fancied and even feared in most cultures and civilizations on the earth. Nonetheless the longing for it by ancient Greeks would barely have resembled the perceived need of it by the ancient Japanese.

Then a cosmic act brought separate individuality and separate personality into being.[3] This was irreversible. <u>Right away critical spirit also came into being</u>. Along with the hoped-for salvation arrived also the potential desolation.

There we have the structure against which resurrected men and women create their eligibility for the new reality. Those who are neither resurrected nor set aside from among those

---

[1] I say inadvertently, because this penchant for criticism is brought to our attention from without, when we notice that once again we <u>have been</u> critical.
[2] Christian Bible, Mt. 10:34.
[3] While we know that 'all was divided', even head from heart, we let those two, individuality / personality, for the time being, serve as examples.

who by comparison are betimes referred to as 'the dead', make their own arrangements 'for the time being', which may be called the modern time.

*

Criticism is abominable. Someone who has tasted human freedom (not merely liberty) is bound to detest criticism. Someone who has a good notion of what true humanity might amount to, cannot but find criticism abhorrent because it precisely denies that humanity. Ethical creation is the work for those who espouse real human being, while criticism, or the critical spirit, tends to undermine all such work.

We can certainly state more clearly now that the folk-spirit is especially aware of this 'abomination that brings on desolation'; of the dehumanization, this distancing from the human soul which, as a result, is <u>sidelined</u>. During our development we may gradually be able to come to terms with the spirit of criticism. If we are in the possession of a folk soul this criticism is foisted upon us rather suddenly due to our innate evolution. The contrast between the malignancy and what we gain by 'pressing past it' into true reality can be rather dramatic.

The tragedy of modern man is that he tries to accommodate critical spirit and to enlist it as a tool in aid of gaining knowledge and understanding. Subsequently he has to be rescued from without, if at all, after an existence riven by uncertainty and strife. [1]

*

---

[1] The tragedy of the modern Faust, in Goethe's work by that name, is that he never gets around to a critique of the critical spirit, and therefore neither to truly good works that would succeed such a critique, and so he struggles forever in terms of that malignant deposit in himself which exists due to, and is, his intercourse with critical spirit, (Mephistopheles).

40

We may assume we have done ourselves some critical damage. A deposit of criticism, or a critical deposit, due to more or less conscious interaction with the critical spirit, may be assumed by us once we consider ourselves to be adult human beings. In the modern world, within a modern environment, we live to an extent in crisis. All that initially separates us from those who embrace that modernity wholeheartedly is our confession of 'the fact' that evidence of the cosmic crisis affects us, even though we do not choose to have any direct access to it and cannot readily relate to it.

It would be inappropriate, wrong and unjust to pass judgment, either on ourselves or on others, on account of something that could not, after all, have been entirely avoided. There is, however, this and that which we can do to make it less likely that we ourselves will choose to exist and behave critically and that others will choose to do so. It comes down to that, after all. To put it as simply and creatively as possible, our attention is inadvertently drawn, by critical spirit, to the germinal separateness of individuality and personality within us and we may choose to behave appropriately, which is to say creatively. That we understand critical spirit as the negative indicator of our great advantage and that we no longer take up with it as though it were an epistemological tool, that is what counts.

*

Criticism affects us indirectly. Reflection is required from us if we are to make sense of it. In short, it is what we suppose others mean that affects us critically. We have no right to insist that they actually mean it. No evidence can be brought up in court to prove that someone has criticized us. Nonetheless the flame has seared us; the heat has singed us. And this is the real evidence and the only evidence that should concern us – which is evidence that once again we may move forward, we may progress in the only true sense of the word – in terms of our resurrection. (Which is certainly not to suggest that we have to wait for evidence.) All that we mean by ethical action and ethical behaviour will follow from this our decision to do good rather than to be critical or to criticize. Criticism affects us inadvertently. As soon as we turn to it to take issue with it we lose our advantage and – become modern. For but one example, we judge so as not to be judged.[1] Or we take the criticism to heart and so as not to behave vengefully – we timidly collapse before it. Both options are modern and destructive. One is destruction of the other person; the decay is destruction of oneself. Revenge and cowardice. So much of modern life consists of those two non-choices played off against each other, whether in politics or in any of the institutionalized pastimes that hog the limelight of the day.

What all we can do – how we can act and behave instead of taking issue with instances of critical spirit, I have delineated in some detail in a separate book.[2] This present essay concerns especially those who choose to wait rather than to follow. Folk-spirit and folk-nature are discrete in essence, even like human spirit and human nature, of which they are a species and to which we compare them.

We may remind ourselves here of an exchange, in the Christian Bible, between Jesus and Peter near the end of the Gospel according to John. Peter has been told three times: "Feed my sheep." He senses that John, "the disciple whom Jesus loved", is somehow in a different category to himself in consideration of work to be done after Jesus has departed. "What shall this man do?" he asks, and Jesus answers: "If I will that he tarry till I come, what is that to thee? Follow thou me." John is to wait.

---

[1] Christian Bible, Mat. 7:1.
[2] 'Travel Notes and Way Stations – a rational ethic'

We get the impression that John's being, his faithful, loving being, is what will count more than anything he specifically does in terms of what Jesus meant by 'feeding his sheep'. Later his watchword, as we know, will be: "Children, love one another." Peter, by comparison, has a resurrection to go through – or at least to complete. He will "turn", he will be converted, and then he will do the work that is cut out, or laid on, for him.[1] It also makes sense that the 'beloved disciple', John, is the writer of the fourth Gospel inasmuch as he does not collate recalled or recorded data but he speaks from within, as from a dream messianically inspired. He is one of those who 'sees visions and dreams dreams'.[2]

*

The one who espouses folk-spirit is not tempted to react to critical spirit. He is set aside from birth. He does not develop and consequently creativity and resurrection, as we shall see, have a character of their own in his case. However he is to evolve. He does not participate in the modern world in the same way and is rarely attached to it, so he sees little need to protect himself against it. However he has his own peculiar problems. Needless to say, he cannot persist in duality. Although he is not tempted to react to critical spirit, he is for that very reason liable to ignore his dualistic state and to try to live either by folk-spirit or in line with folk-nature. It is from what happens to him when he makes such attempts that he must take his evolutionary cue.

When he tries to live by folk-spirit alone, his nature decays; not he but his nature. When he tries to live in line with his folk-nature – soon it is no longer his nature.

---

[1] Christian Bible, Jn: 21:18.
[2] Christian Bible, Acts 2:17.

43

So the danger of the one who is set aside is that he will become <u>dispirited or denatured</u>. What he waits for therefore, and
what he is wise to wait for, is that the two, time and again, <u>will
become one</u>. Of course the waiting he does is neither unconscious nor unaware. It is simply a <u>waiting in faith</u>. (This is what
Jesus meant by tarrying.) He knows he is 'set aside' for a purpose which will become clear to him. When it does, his first
task is then a <u>critique of critical spirit</u>. While he waits, or tar-
ries, this spirit takes no interest in him because during that time
he presents no danger to the status quo. He does not interfere
with 'the ancient lay of the land'. A soon as he comes out of
himself in order to make his germinal contribution to his community, he is a threat to the status quo and immediately finds
that his character is being challenged. We may also turn it
around and say that as soon as his being is challenged he may
know that the time has come for him to engage productively
with that disturbance – unless he behaves like Young Werther
in Goethe's story and succumbs, dispirited.

*

This story, 'the Sufferings of the young Werther', is itself of
course Goethe's own critique of the critical spirit, which he
undertakes and by which he highlights the massive landscape
of 'ancient' sentiment that confronts the contemporary soul,
which 'hopes' not to be modernized. One-sided indulgence in
that 'landscape' is a recipe for trouble and we are grateful to any
creative genius who draws these dangers to our attention in some
acceptable form. And by the way, this is precisely what we
mean by genius, that even the elemental depth and breadth of
contemporary reality is facilitated and dignified for 'consump-
tion in the light of day'.

The critical spirit typically would drive true human beings to
suicide. It is near impossible, during a materialistic epoch, to

take such a mythic entity as the critical spirit seriously as something to be confronted. As a consequence the materialistic status quo remains de facto unchallenged until once again a major critique manages to capture the imagination of a sizeable segment of the population.

At the time in Europe when such books as Rousseau's 'La Nouvelle Héloïse' and Goethe's 'Leiden des Jungen Werther' managed to make their mark, the status quo was not materialistic but theologically conservative and equally uncreative, like every comfortable status quo.

A critique of critical spirit indirectly alerts us to our powerful creative faculties – or else condemns us for not coming up with any. Once we realize that this spirit's task may even be to 'sift us like wheat'[1] we may fall back on our faith and allow ourselves to be sifted, perhaps as we record that process in some way, or simply describe it or portray it for others who might be afraid. We may well, during that trying time, find ourselves in a desert of sorts but we can draw on the wisdom of those who came before us. We may not belong to a tradition that allows us to counteract the critical spirit's arguments with: "It is written..." [2] but the Gospels themselves contain a marvellous amount of useful wisdom to help us deal with every crisis in our life.

*

The specific character of folk spirit, in comparison to human spirit (of which it is an example) becomes plain in terms of the approach to the crisis directly brought about by the achievement of Jesus of Nazareth. This crisis was experienced directly by Paul of Tarsus, who after his conversion fought hard for the acceptance of his particular teaching of the dying and living

---

[1] Christian Bible, Lk. 22:31.
[2] Christian Bible, Mt. 4:1-11.

45

again of Jesus within those who were baptized. At the same
time there were those who needed to understand what was going on within them, upon baptism, indirectly. By baptism I
mean what happens to us due to the spirit of truth finding acceptance within us, either due to true words spoken or read or
due to some ritual act by someone who is informed and actually inhabited by the spirit of truth. Jesus himself performed
many of such ritual acts, devised on the spur of the moment to
suit someone who was to be healed by his faith. His words
cleanse the apostles. He also delivers the spoken truth either
directly or indirectly as parables, as stories, or a good advice
which he calls 'his commandments'. These commandments
are, however, of the nature: 'If you hope to weather the crisis,
you will have to behave and think like this and like that, and
not like the other. Much of both his direct and indirect prepara-
tion for the crisis is of the nature of a cleansing, so that some at
least will make it into the new reality rather than being pre-
vented by unsuitable attachments and inappropriate ways of
feeling, thinking and habits of behaviour.

What I mean by the folk-spirit is therefore the spirit of those
who have weathered the crisis – (who have managed the transition from the old to the new, from this world to the kingdom of
heaven, or however else we might be able to describe this tran-
substantiation) – indirectly and who therefore exist in this new
reality entirely in terms of what they believe on the basis of a
consummation of common sense. They are not to be moved by
theology nor stopped by criticism. They simply accept and have
no need to overcome.

The transition for all is from old to new, from ancient to contemporary.

The folk-nature is a human nature of which the bearer of
folk-spirit is only indirectly aware. Therefore he should not be

46

expected to understand what it means to have "the dying and living again of Christ within us", nor should we ask him to perform ethical deeds that depend upon his cooperation with his soul. Creation such as that arises from an <u>understanding</u> of merciful good spirit, in addition to believing, knowing and loving.

All who are touched directly or indirectly by the truth and respond truthfully, either press into this new order of being where eternal life is available – or they live in it, eternally, and work to bring others in.

No one today who has at least a taste of real life is going to be disturbed much either by those who deny merciful good spirit or those who set up some idol in the place of it.

There is a certain kind of help that those who espouse the folk spirit need from those who understand the ins and outs of the commonwealth of reality and that is the definition of the critical spirit. They cannot come to terms with it themselves, so at times they are liable to be only folk-natural or only folk-spiritual, and this is a confusion for them and it causes them pain – not to mention the pain it causes those around them. In other words, the critical spirit is a danger to them as to all of us if we do not understand the purpose of it, however this danger cannot be identified by them, so they are liable to initiate evasive moves that cause them more harm than good.

The one who understands is able to help the one who is not capable of understanding by translating concepts into images. Folk-spirit readily deals in images while concepts as such are rejected because inappropriate. While the one who understands must deal in concepts so as to deliver himself from the critical spirit, such as during the course of a critique, the one who is set aside must be supplied with appropriate images, both if his being has become unbalanced and if he is to sustain the balance of his being.

Remember that folk-spirit and folk-nature are the two sides of human being specifically in the absence of outward, creative-ethical action as such

Now while these 'specialists' of being need the help of those who "are familiar with the <u>household of the true reality</u>" so as not to mistake the critical spirit and possibly take up with it, those, in turn, who are at home in the kingdom do well to enlist the help of those who are familiar with the <u>household of the earth</u>, namely those whose folk-nature is endowed with folk-spirit.

If that does not make for a marriage made in heaven, I would like to know what does.

*

Let us consider the <u>folk-soul</u> now, as possessed by the one whose folk-nature and folk-spirit are in balance or equipoise. He does not react to his soul but is liable to lean too much to the left or the right, to his nature or to spirit, and when he notices this – or when this is brought to his notice – he waits faithfully for the balance to re-establish itself.

Just as every resurrectional move is one of cooperation with merciful good spirit as our soul – if we develop and evolve out of our modern condition – so does a <u>tarrying</u> amount to a <u>restitution</u> of the one whose folk-nature and folk-spirit have become to any degree disparate. This word 'tarry', which means to wait, to abide, before doing anything, seems to me to indicate precisely this act of allowing oneself to sink into faith rather than to acting outwardly in faith and I call it a restitution because of what happens as a result, which is that we are 'back home' as it were, and no longer in danger of decay or decline. We are where we wish to be so that we can be, effectively. And a critique of the critical spirit can certainly be well described in this case as effective being. (Remember that when we mainly are, we also do, in the sense that we are also effective, just as when we mainly do we do not cease to be.)

The difference between 'tarrying' and 'following'[1] which I make use of, from the fourth Gospel, to illustrate how we in the modern world might be and behave in order to come around to true reality, highlights two ways of coping with the transition into that realm of the new reality plus the useful behaviour once one has entered and reaches out. Christian theology knows only the resurrection which means something other than an ongoing process which is the existence and growth of a mature human being in community. As soon as we care enough to stand by actual men and women on the earth who experience merciful good spirit in their own way and who need help as they try to come to terms with the manifold demands made on their knowledge and understanding, on their moods, their sanity and their physical wellbeing, it helps us to distinguish between those who respond creatively to their reactions, overcoming whatever crops up between them and their goal, and those who rely directly on their faith to keep them in the fold and effective.

Also we need to keep in mind – if we ourselves want to be effective rather than 'thrashing straw' or simply resting under our halo as 'saved Christians' – that we exist in the modern world and not in the ancient world in which Jesus lived. While Jesus was certainly able to foresee what would vex us moderns, those he taught and advised came up against hindrances with which we can hardly sympathize. All the language readily at our disposal has been influenced by two-thousand years of

---

[1] Between menō and akoloutheō

49

modern feeling and thinking. So, for example, it makes sense that a christianity worth its salt always needs to be reworked but more important is our willingness to learn how to live eternally on the earth, capable of unconditional love and desirous of human communality.

*

It is especially the folk-soul that is to contact ancient reality – that is able to bring us into contact with the ancient life within us, in such a way that it merges with our contemporary life. Modern life stands separate from ancient life and modern man portrays it as something that is dead and gone and needs to be unearthed, disembalmed, archaeologically rediscovered as a dead thing and kept in a specialist box where it can forever be poked at, studied and argued over. As moderns, we need the ancients for comparison and contrast, to help us sustain ourselves as moderns in case true reality should intervene.

The folk-soul precisely is not modern. It encourages us, urges and prompt us, to match the ancient with the contemporary reality. It is not a link between the ancient world and the modern world that is required, but an increasingly rich contemporary reality that recognizes no barrier, artificial or otherwise, between the old and the new. The modern pseudo-reality cannot help but produce a modern past and a modern future, on account of the modern present that is viewed and experienced as a legitimate thing in itself.

A critique of the critical spirit is the folk-soul's initial activity. It is the critical spirit that placates modernity in all its various insistences on itself and where modernity is praised the critical spirit does the praising. Meanwhile that part of our soul that is the folk-soul (think of it like that for the moment) immerses itself in faith in order to comply with the irritations, the provocations, the insults and outright attacks on itself by the critical spirit. It complies in the sense that it understands the modern influence, whether that influence originates in modern individuals or in ordinary materialistic or spiritualistic conditions. Modern circumstances, we do best not to forget, are largely inventions and productions of critical spirit and we may as well admit that we cannot avoid being affected. Certainly we should not go out of our way to participate in modern circumstances. On the other hand it would not do us much good to try to protect ourselves against these circumstances or to try to get rid of them. What would we prefer?

What counts therefore is that we remain aware of our power to be faithful. That way we will not lose courage and we will not be tempted to criticize.

This is where our intellect comes into its own. Intellectually we can define every crisis: every intrusion into our wellbeing, every impertinence that questions our sanity, every impropriety that calls our ultimate ability into question – before we hand ourselves over, so to speak, to our truthful soul. Thereupon it is given to us either to do or else to refrain from doing. As we become experts in this field, we notice that the definition of the crisis and the handing of ourselves over to faith in practice coincide. Certainly we need practice at this. There will be no shortage of opportunity, we may take that for granted. Time and again we notice that we criticize back instead of tarrying and practicing the necessary critique.

I suppose the first and most important discipline would hinge upon any habit we are in to criticize in the first place. Our folk-soul will not allow that. Mercifully such errors are quickly brought home to us, albeit painfully. Let us not misunderstand the pain. And that includes that familiar gleefulness when we notice that someone is trapped in the error we ourselves have only just then avoided. 'There she is, indulging herself in her crazy half hour again," the long-suffering husband thinks, little realizing how guilty he is of neglect. Every opportunity for being faithful under duress that we neglect really amounts to a loss of power.

And why do we need the power? We need it for the work we are going to do. What will be the nature of the work? It will exemplify the folk-soul. And what is the essence of the folk-soul? It is unity, oneness and completeness within.

Now if we ask the next owner of a folk-soul not what he believes is the essence of his work – because we know that already – but rather how he intends to be of use to his community, he will say: "Let me think. It has to come from me, what I do. It must not be a copy of what anyone else is doing or has done, that is crucial. Of course I may respond to a plea by someone who would like something done, however in that case his request will have to be presented in the most general of terms because here too I must be free to spin my own cocoon, to build my nest to comfort myself and to draw my own lines in the sand beyond which I shall not step. Then again someone in the midst of despair will look upon me and hope to receive a kindness and what I shall do or refrain from doing will depend entirely on the productive power of my sympathy and not at all on what anyone in that position might expect. Then again, if someone is nasty to me or plain inconsiderate, I will use my power to render myself incapable of reaction and show my faith in the light of day. Not up to me to correct, to check, to alter. If the desire to do so should surface in me, my task will be to critique the critical spirit within me, where somehow it has managed to gain a foothold."

*

What does it mean, that we have ancient life within us? Surely we are no longer attached to what we have left behind.

52

True, but that is why we have ready access to it for our work. In terms of our folk-soul we allow ourselves to be moved by that which existed prior to the modern era, which is ancient.

The modern era, after all, is nothing substantial. Once we are in touch with true reality, we no longer think in terms of it. It is a thing, a historic thing, if you like, concocted by modern minds. So finally what we have is these two: ancient time, prior to the achievement of Jesus of Nazareth, and true reality, in which time is eternal.

What is modernity after all except a culpable reluctance to let go of the ancient presuppositions, the ancient massive thing-culture? Mind you, things as compared to beings did not step onto the stage until the division due to the Christ took place. So surely it is our reluctance to know ourselves as truly divided that we should think about when we wonder about modernity. It is the fear of this discreteness of our two halves, over the joining of which our religious work is to begin. What we fear mostly is the guilt and shame for having neglected our work for so long. How silly!

This is surely what we come up against during every crisis, that there is no going back, only a seeing it through or getting stuck in it. What we mean here is a growth crisis; a developmental or evolutionary crisis. We cannot step back from it, take another look before we decide to commit. No, we are in it, involved whether we like it or not and we have only the two choices: intelligent perseverance or cowardly dithering. And sadly we have greater proof than ever nowadays that we can dither with a vengeance.

One silly way to try to avoid that unkindly cut within that we mentioned earlier is to gather in crowds on starboard or on the port side of the ship. What might that lead to? There are so many. And a storm is brewing. The folk-spirit of the one who is dispirited, if he chooses to continue to be so rather than immersing himself in faith, will continue to weigh him down, to depress him, to make him suppose he has no friends and to draw him into various activities that will confirm him in a state of desuetude, which is to say he increasingly feels he is no use on the earth and he tends to suicide. If anyone suggest to him he 'should' be doing one thing or the other, this increases his malaise because things, for one thing, disenchant him at the very time when he seems to wish he were enchanted, that is to say, when he seeks out magical solutions to his predicament. Drugs are readily abused in the hope that they will supply that magic. On the other hand he cannot abide being forced into situations that are intended to give him a taste of usefulness because any kind of force brings on the existential despair out of which only death release him.

All this time the critical spirit is having its way with him. Those of us who suppose we might be able to help someone in this condition might as well make ourselves aware of how the critical spirit highlights the individual weaknesses of such a person, so that – seen from the point of view of merciful good spirit – the afflicted one will be aided by someone who knows what is going on and makes no attempts at a cure by means of modern medication. Such medication does not apply to the archetypical modern ailments.

The dispirited individual has no access to his folk-soul. At least he does not choose to turn to it. It might be best not to take for granted that he does have access, because if we do and we are wrong we only succeed in aggravating his deplorable condition. What can we do help him, that is the question. The illusion that we know better because we are not depressed at the time may at once be declared null and void. All that we need to ask ourselves is: Are we in possession of our soul? Do we know the difference between psyche and soul?

Is ours not psyche but soul? If we know of no difference, we may forget trying to help someone. We are bound to do more damage than good. What is needed is true compassion. Not the word but the deed is needed. We may search in ourselves for our soul and once we have found it we have what it takes to help that individual. Now all we need to do is remain in possession of our soul, whatever else we do. We may try involve that individual in conversation, we may ask will he go for a walk with us, we may ask him questions or wait for him to ask us questions; we may read to him, let him read to us, take him to a concert or join him in making some Christmas presents for the poor and needy. None of that is useful if in the meantime we are not patiently in the possession of our soul – for his sake. It is that we do it for his sake that alone makes it work. (Imagine trying to achieve such a thing for money!) Probably we will find ourselves having to do it again and again, especially if we are not in the habit of practicing compassion.

If this were not downright impossible for so many, one would feel inclined to say: Goodness me, is that all there is to it? However we have in mind that soul is not modern. Can we indeed lay aside our modernity for the time it takes to help someone return to what is essential for him as a human being? Modernity thrives on evidence: there is no evidence for our soul. How do you know, they will say, that you have one? It is when you ask yourself: 'Do I have a soul?', then you will know. A soul is truthful, certain and above all else eager to impart itself where a soul is wanted.

Our soul is merciful good spirit of love within us, eager to leap any critical barrier between ourselves and two or three other human beings.

*

55

Those sightseers who all rush to starboard may be described as <u>denatured</u> rather than dispirited. Now someone who is denatured is not in possession of his soul either but his condition differs somewhat from that of the dispirited one in that he continually strives to augment his standing vis-à-vis the status quo. Thereby he plays right into the hands of the critical spirit, which does, as we know, stand for that status. He will knock himself out trying to fit in. He will forever be looking for recognition and praise. Also he will be most singularly unwilling, practically incapable, of suffering criticism.

The denatured individual has no soul yet but quite often he is abundantly endowed with psychic characteristics, psychic weakness and psychic strengths. Happily the way he presents these characteristics cannot suit the status quo. I say happily, because if they did, would he not trade in his potential for soul in favour of modernism? So his works are rejected and he himself is shunned. As a consequence he tends to hysteria and to hypocrisy. In this way he wants to force or seduce the status quo to take note of him and to reward him with some of the glittering prizes of the modern world. Once again, however the modern experts will say: "No, you do not have it right quite yet. You are closer than ever but there is much work to do." And so on. Possibly he will catch on now and realize that the solution to what ails him rests within him and not with the extinct status quo. If he does not, we may ask ourselves what we can do for him.

It is in fact very unlikely that he will, from himself, arrive at the necessary solution. This is because of something like an addiction to praise, and to criticism too. Our addictions need to be brought to our attention from outside, that is unavoidable. So what we might be able to do for someone is the following. Whenever the criticism of the denatured one is in full swing we might simply turn to our soul in order to persist at as great a distance from the critical spirit as possible, without taking issue

56

with the criticism directed at us and hopefully without criticizing back. We can do the same to rid ourselves of the annoyance when someone unduly praises us, for the reason of getting the better of us. However the actual failing of the one who is denatured is his lack of true confidence because time again he insists on self-confidence.

Now we know that self-confidence depends on approval and praise from outside, in the present case on recognition from those who stand for the status quo; also for the critical spirit, which is the supposed saviour of the status quo and of those who swear by the status quo. The most abhorrent judgments are made, as we know, on behalf of the status quo and the critical Christ, so that we find ourselves turning away in horror, possibly aggravating the situation for ourselves instead of looking for something we might do to ameliorate the situation for the one caught up in this nonsense.

Possibly the best medicine in this case is to boost the affected person's true confidence while ignoring or side-stepping self-confidence. This means, first of all, that we have to be perfectly clear in our own minds about the difference between the two. Critical spirit as the antichrist is no picnic to deal with. Never has there been, nor will there be, greater need for wisdom than in the presence of the antichrist, precisely because we ourselves, whatever we may suppose at times, are susceptible. We know that the critical spirit stepped into the breach as soon as the breach was made due to Christ's achievement. Equally does it step into the breach whenever we ourselves make a wounding remark, or cut someone from the effect of our good will, or behave insolently. Sadly we ourselves, on a day to day basis, make allowances for the antichrist, not because of something we do so much as on account of what we neglect to do – which is to 'make the two one'. What is this antichrist after all, if we look at it sub specie aeternitatis, but the crucial reminder that is to set us on the course of truth and personal reality again. What is modernity except all the bad examples and critical assumptions against which we can sort ourselves out.

The spirit of true confidence, on which we would like to depend and of which we would like to set an example specifically for the one who is caught up in some denaturing condition, is always accessible to us from within in terms of some actual reliance, by us, on its formative principle. It suffices that we wish to be confident for the purpose of helping someone who is unconfident. That is how the spirit of comfort and confidence works. In order to rise within us it needs to flow through us and it can only do that if our intention is to help someone who has become fatigued by endless criticism or by striving to avoid criticism by playing into the hands of the status quo – which, of course, is itself the creation of critical spirit.

Even as our main desire is always to strengthen those who lack the confidence to break away from adherence to critical spirit, so we must guard ourselves against making something out of this 'status quo' which it is not. It is not this or that. If we want once and for all time to settle down in some realm or dominion or personal state in which we will no longer have to be creative and depending on faith, then ours is a desire for the status quo. It matters little whether this desire stems from tiredness or from zealotry; whether we are dispirited or denatured, the result is the same. The desire itself is critical and we ourselves who desire will be critical of anyone and anything that urges or prompts us to believe in truth or to create truthfully.

As a matter of fact, all through the modern centuries, has there ever been a time when the populations of the earth did not picture some supernatural realm in the future when all would be decided once and for all and no one would be left to argue against the good ones because they would be justified for all time? This supernatural realm, so frequently mistaken for the 'Kingdom of God' by various Christian religions, is so far wide of the mark that we can readily identify it as a concoction of the critical spirit, which by definition finds everything 'wanting' that demands a degree even of intelligent suffering or of preventative creativity. And all those who, during those centuries, have identified the antichrist as this or that ruler, secular or religious, are merely being critical of their entire environment, otherwise why would they not simply refer it to themselves as that which is given them to deal with, to revive or simply to ignore? No, they have misled thousands in their efforts to prove themselves to finally have been the ones to have belled the cat and now we can all relax and be happy. The original author of that term 'antichrist' seems to me to be at least sensible in the way he uses it. Then, as the criticism accumulates and modern media amass, Christendom becomes the actual status quo for those on the western slopes of the globe and those who disagree are crucified, burned and incarcerated. What a very gradual passage it has been for the truth!

Those with a folk-soul should really be in the forefront when it comes to an understanding of where the critical shoe pinches. They have the immediate access to the truth and there is no reason for them to bandy words and concepts with the theological technicians or to knock themselves out in terms of the modern Sciences. Among human beings, who all have a soul, they are the ones to bring confidence and comfort on one side and compassion on the other – once they are established in themselves and no longer indecisive.

Their works – and there is no reason why we should not call them works even though they are ontologically determined – can not be undermined or overlooked. Once these works are out in the open they operate ineluctably. They are effective because they are and their effect touches beings. We may say they are simply affective. Not the originator of these works but the works themselves create – and this is a distinction which helps us make use of whatever works we come across and we contemplate making use of them or letting them affect us. So for example we read the Gospel of Mark and time after time we settle back and reflect on what we have read. We turn various passages this way and that way, we recall how we understood them once and compare this how we understand them now. We may memorize certain passages, so that in our time of extremity we are supplied, as it were, with emergency rations, in the depth of despair or on the height of self-approval. Most of all we come across passages the meaning of which may well be otherwise presented in the other two synoptic Gospels, so we compare and coordinate until we come upon that which is of use to us at that time. So we would not, for example, argue about which passage is correct, more original or less doctrinal. All that matters to us is does it 'answer', does it hold water and help us get out of the fire. Can we drink it, eat it, and will it keep us warm.

If that was all we had, we would be richly rewarded. We would not suppose that we need anything else and our gratitude would have no bounds.

However in addition to the synoptic Gospels we have the Gospel of John, and John's folk-soul leaves us in no doubt about how we should approach this book. In fact we do not approach it at all, if we know what we are doing, because an approach implies a gradually increasing interest and a slowly growing familiarity. This is however the way to read the synoptic Gospels. The fourth Gospel is a bath in the truth. It is an intentional cleansing of ourselves of all that, unbeknownst to ourselves, stands in our way and has been moved by us and allowed to accumulate by us to stand in the way to our enjoyment of the true and eternal life. Here in this Gospel the speeches of Jesus are such as to infiltrate rather than excite our intellect, such as to organize our knowledge and understanding rather than to persuade us to plan and control it.

*

I have elsewhere in my work identified what I called <u>sacramental influence</u> that arrives with us from without. This influence is merciful good spirit direct into our system. If we know about it, we may open ourselves to it. If we do not know about it, nothing is gained and nothing lost. One of the great and singular advantages of a folk-soul is that it is in fact open to sacramental influence from birth and only if during our life we close ourselves to it by becoming one-sided, as I have described it, do we become sacramentally inert – which is then experienced, naturally or spiritually, as a spectacular shortcoming. A dispirited individual will seem to himself like a motherless child, in need of the most fundamental protection, while the denatured one will be like the son of man and have nowhere to rest his head. We who are sacramentally adept can therefore be of especial help to the one-sided ones by introducing them to our sacramental being – our being inasmuch as it broadcasts the very wellbeing of our close familiarity with merciful good spirit. They will not know enough to look for this advantage but they will have the benefit of it all the same.

*

It is difficult to estimate ahead of time what all we can do to help a 'one-sided one'. Our nature is so inventive in coming up with hindrances when we do not supply the necessary cooperation. We may suppose we understand all that I put forward here, but when we stand in front an actual human being, especially a young one, we are stumped. Now begins the work of sympathy, of empathy and compassion. Now it helps us immensely if we are able to rely on the effect of our sacramental being. We have endless time as soon as we realize that the onus is on us to bring about a beneficial change in someone. Now and again it may be important to keep in mind that we will not be thanked directly by that person for any good we do. So it might help us, since we have become so dependent upon visible results in our customary modernity, to consider now and again how much good we do ourselves by doing someone else good. However we have to be solidly established in ourselves if this is not to undermine our initial intention hypocritically. Finally the sure way forward allows us to ignore all notions of reward.

*

Throughout this essay I have distinguished between the creative soul and the faithful soul. My reason for doing so is not to be able to say that one human being has a faithful soul and the other a creative one, but rather to learn about what it means to have a soul and to realize that from one person to the next the emphasis may change, more on creativity or more on faithfulness.

Creativity implies the overcoming of a hindrance. When we create, we understand that whatever bothers us does so, in a word, for our own good, and then we set about to prove it. When we are creative, our attitude to our mortality is one of gratitude and our immortality we take for granted.

Faithfulness on the other hand implies a being more than a doing. We are faithful, and out of this faithfulness rise various advantages both for others and for ourselves. Any difference between mortality and immortality does not really concern us all that much because we know we have what it takes to be in god and we live eternally.

There are those whose soul is both faithful and creative in equal capacity but mostly one or the other is greater.

Possession of soul implies merciful good spirit, or god, accessible within us. How we come into the possession of our soul, that is one story. So much hinges on the extent to which we are committed to modern thought processes and convictions, all of which, by definition, are either energized or inhibited by criticism. I have identified the critical spirit as the 'abomination of desolation', and as that which steps into the breach caused by the cosmic achievement of Jesus of Nazareth[1] – and also as that which draws our attention to the need for faith and creative action.

When we find ourselves in a crisis, the best way to stay in it is to criticize. The best way to get out of it is faithfully or creatively; the two overlap. The cosmic crisis of mankind can be described in any number of ways but what characterizes it from the start is that the truth is no longer a matter of appearances and that reality <u>as we find</u> it has no single, unified meaning. The notion of permanence in daily life, like the calculation of historic credibility and what is meant by process and measurement, is so thoroughly based on ideas, that in our modern skins we can no longer move or breathe. The fact that the divine substance has entered flesh and blood can be ignored but not with impunity. We can press into the kingdom of heaven or go down with depression. We can learn to suffer intelligently and grow or be overwhelmed by sickness and disease.

One initial approach that will open our eyes to the seriousness of the modern dilemma is a critique of critical spirit, beginning always with the malignant deposit within us due to our intercourse with critical spirit. What we need to understand there, is that we have to assume responsibility even for the unavoidable initial reaction to critical spirit, not to mention any subsequent intercourse by choice. If we would still like to make

---

[1] It 'ought not' to step into the breach because we ourselves, during the course of our resurrection, belong there, faithful and truly creative.

use of the word 'sin', then we might usefully define it as the unwillingness to take that responsibility. Negligence in this department from birth to death is entirely feasible. On the other hand, if we want to make a start, we have to accept that god is on our side, that divine spirit is merciful and actually willing for us to mature. The first sign of this willingness is Jesus of Nazareth as divinely human (or humanly divine). The second sign is that we ourselves are able to take the fullest possible advantage of this first sign, by loving and believing in this god plus Jesus as spiritually present within us. The third sign is that we are actually drawn by experience to this eternal order, in other words by all the aches and pain, the troubles and inconveniences, the illnesses and insanities that visit us during the course of our existence. All our afflictions mean that salvation is on the cards for us; or expressing this in contemporary language, all our afflictions are growing-pains and the growth is joyful if we suffer the pain intelligently. Lastly, the ability to read these three signs is a gift of god and no one can force us to see the sense of them.

*

A critique is a sorting out of the grain from the chaff, of the illusion from the substance and of the meaning from the nonsense. So what exactly is a critique of the critical spirit? What we are looking at is our own involvement with critical spirit and the supposed cause of that involvement, that intercourse, as we called it earlier. We will try to come to terms with that aspect of the spirit that seems attractive to us because it persuades us to see ourselves as in total control of our existence and as totally independent from all other beings. Once we understand this we will respond to it by relying on our folk soul. The outcome of this will be mostly our behaviour, but perhaps a work, or even just a demonstration of how to be free of critical spirit.

64

We cannot imagine, literally we cannot, what it is like for someone in our vicinity when we are critical. We behave like we owned the earth. Cooperation with anyone else is out of the question. We give cryptic instructions and expect that person to know what we mean, to understand our purpose. If they show any doubt, any uncertainty as to how they should follow our instructions, we become impatient to the point of wanting to destroy them. "Here, give me that! Go away! Why can you not just do what I say! You are stupid. I have defined myself as the one who knows and can do everything. Why do you question that? Yes, you do, you do question it. Is it so difficult just to accept that you are a mere extension of my unreasonable and intolerant will?" Like that.

Then we harbour all that resentment if it after all becomes impossible for us to rule the world.

If instead of acting out our malignancy we were to practice a critique of it, we would realize that those around us would suddenly turn into quite cooperative, cheerful, friendly companions who were able to guess what we wanted before we did. Instead they shy away from us. They close as many doors as possible between us and them. When they run out of doors they just play dead. Here, I am a mere lump of clay. Form me to your pleasure. I realize you must be God. You what? You want me to show some initiative? Never heard of it.

There is no way of getting around it, the critical person is demonic. Even the resentment is demonic. He or she is possessed by a demon that whispers into his or her ear: 'No one else knows but you. Now impress your egotistic self on all your surroundings. Turn all those in your vicinity into abject doubles of your self. If this does not work, let them feel what you think of them.

This, after all, is what it means to be demonic. The self comes out of itself. It ravages the environment. It strikes terror into the population. Not that it means to do that. If 'everyone' just quietly were to relinquish their being – yes, their being, that's it – then there would be no need for ravaging, for terror, for a fight as big as a row.

A critique then seeks to establish – and to re-establish – being. Since being is the pronounced, formative intention of the folk-spirit, we can surely understand how we, who are endowed specifically with our folk-soul, need to learn how to practice a critique. It shall be a critique of the demonic malignancy within ourselves. This is a tremendous skill. If someone else in our vicinity is just now laying this malignancy on, we do not really know this – not really – until we are somewhat affected by it. Then that is the time for us to exercise critique-leverage. "Here it is," we then say to ourselves, reflectively. "This is it. Time to do it now. Waste no time. Get down to it. Take your eyes, your ears, your everything entirely off that other one who seems to be raising cane and creating havoc and concentrate on what only you can do." You take issue with the malignancy in yourself. You notice how our own self wants to begin to cut a caper. You say no to that. You say No! No! And you might be able to leave it at that, if you are superbly practiced at this business of 'casting out demons'. This ancient expression is not so far-fetched now, is it. Suddenly we understand a bit better what Jesus of Nazareth did when he 'healed people'. What he actually did, as we can make out when we take a closer look, is that he vanquished the present demon, even as he noted it in himself, compassionately, and then he encouraged the afflicted one to sink into his or her faith. "Have faith!" "Your faith has made you well."

Our faithful being is interrupted by that critical malignancy. No being – no faith! No faith – no being! Suddenly no critical spirit – now both faith and being.

"Have faith!" we say to the afflicted one. However if that afflicted one labours under the shadow of that deposit of malignancy within himself, faith even as a distant possibility is nowhere in sight. Ah, we say, let us tell you about faith. It is the faith of the orthodox Christian. You must believe this and that and the other. You must take a leap of faith. There is nothing for it, you must do as I say. There is no hope for you otherwise. I might even go ahead now and abuse you, for your own good, of course, so that you get the hang of this, just repeat after me the following articles of faith and repeat them often to ourself, and badger your children into saying them often until their very childish heads are full of them. Otherwise how can we all be Christians and be happy with that particular status quo? Alright then, if you don't like these Christian beliefs, try these Muslim ones, or the Catholic ones, or maybe try Judaism. Be a Buddhist or a Hindu, heavens, from the point of view of my demonic persuasion I don't care what your beliefs are as long as you have beliefs. It helps if you have a holy book to back them up: the Torah, the Bible, the Koran etc. etc. and if you say anything bad about any of those books your head is coming off, I'm not joking.

"Ah," we say, "let us tell you again about the need to have a faith." And before you can say knife the evangelism has become demonic. There is no quicker way to destroy someone's faith than to persuade him to have a faith. What we do to our children by inculcating in them a faith is unbelievable. We destroy their being – including their ability to be faithful.

So have faith. Learn to trust your folk-soul. Practice being faithful, especially at that moment when you are in doubt which way to lean, left or right. Identify the folk-spirit within you. That is the spirit you have thanks to Jesus of Nazareth and your folk-nature is he. Oh what power you have suddenly! Such joy wells up in you, because now you know. --- Then comes the desolation. "I have lost my faith, woe is me!" you cry. This is abominable! How can you lose your faith? *Your* faith? You have lost it? Here, have mine. It's well worn in and it never wears out. Try to remember now what we said about the need to practice that critique of the critical spirit within you. When you said: "I have lost my faith," you were being critical, of yourself, in that malignant way. (Please don't resent me for saying so.) That was the start. Now the abomination of desolation is standing where it ought not. Don't panic. "Blessed is he that waits,"[1] says the prophet Daniel. And the apostle John, the one who, according to Jesus, was to 'tarry', mentions nothing of this abomination which all three of the synoptic Gospel writers mention, which does not surprise us. He is especially gifted with the ability to wait. Keep in mind that modernity is our visitation, is our affliction, our trial. The German translation for visitation, affliction, trial is *Heimsuchung*, literally a home-seeking. That places the emphasis 'where it ought'. Let's not get hysterical. Let's try to avoid as much hypocrisy as possible. Scare-mongering about the so-called end-time destroys any remnant of faith and increases the demonic terror and resentment. I now we do not practice a thoroughgoing critique, we will allow these scare-mongers and end-time enthusiasts and abomination of desolation-fanatics to fill our heads with tinsel and our hearts with the offal of moles.

*

While we are modern we are in crisis.

---

[1] Daniel 12:12

It may be difficult for a lot of us to get our heads around this. Being modern is a very specific predicament. It is, not to mince words, *the* predicament. Let's not pretend that it is just another predicament, alongside not being able to meet the next mortgage payment or not being able to think of a suitable Christmas present for Aunt Mildred. Or let's put it this way: All our predicaments really stem from the main one, which is being modern. (I am taking for granted here that we are all human beings.)

So why not get as wide a range as possible of ways to be modern so that we know better – not how to avoid it, because no one can avoid modernity, but how to use it as a stepping stone once we notice an infection. Yes, it can be an infection, because we live not only among those who are accidentally modern but perhaps mostly among those who choose to be modern. So while we cannot avoid the odd infection – I mean once we have undertaken a once and for all time critique – we can behave in such a way that the infections are minimal and rare – and stepping-stones to more faithful being.

This is what it is about, increased faithful being. We the blessed folk! We know and understand that we cannot really live unless we have a good effect on those around us. Against that, people are never done telling us how to do good and how to be good and we cannot really take to their advice. I wonder why that is. So now that we have tried it often enough we realize that we do good when we are faithfully. Our being then rubs off on others, put it that way. That makes good sense. And whatever makes good sense gives us just that little bit more wellbeing for our body. It all adds up.

Surviving is the same as living, true or false? If you think it's the same, you are modern. If you start supposing there might be a difference and that there might be more to living than surviving you have taken a small step away from modernity in the direction of eternal life. I call it a small step, and it is, but it involves a critique. You cannot just look away from that malignant deposit and hope it will no longer be. No, you have to turn it into faithful being. And you have to find a way of doing that as you yourself can do. There is no universal recipe. How boring if there were, considering that every critique also adds to the general life-interest. I have, during the course of this essay, supplied several critiques. As a matter of fact every such essay is in itself a critique of mine which I offer to you the reader. I have written close to a hundred essays and all of them stem from my turning incurred modernity-infection into faithful being – in print, because I'm a scribe; not a modern scribe, I hasten to add, but a contemporary one. If you are not a contemporary scribe, you will have to find another way of letting us know how you deal with you malignancy. That is how we work in the 'kingdom of heaven' so as to open doors for others who are sick and tired of being modern. I think of 'modern' as a kind of dry rot or mould, a decay of sorts. As a matter of fact, come to think of it, the verb 'módern', in German, with the accent on the first syllable, means just that: to putrefy and moulder. All you have to do is shift the accent to the last syllable and you have modérn, in German, which means modern, or up-do-date, progressive, fashionable, stylish, elegant trendy. Oh my goodness, really? 'Fraid so. It's make-your-mind-up time. Modern or contemporary. Oh, right. So the faithful being you advocate is contemporary? Yes, precisely. An OED definition of contemporary gives us: 'Living, existing or occurring together in time. Simultaneous.' Let us add one small ingredient to suit our folk-soul: *Being* together in time. Not in someone else's notion of time but in time. Not attached to some idea of time but in time. A critique of time reveals it to us as the very ambience of our being on earth. As soon as we step out of that ambience we are in trouble. All we have to do is imagine time as a linear monad and off go all these firecrackers in our brain and we start imagining super-realities. What a waste of good time! Folk will tell you: 'All in good time,' and they mean it. Picture time as a circle, as a snake that bites its own tail and gradually the ground under you feet turns into quicksand. Why is that now, I wonder. Well, let's not waste time worrying about it. When we suppose there's not enough time to bathe the baby before dinner time, that's one thing, but when we feel, really feel, a shortage of time, a scarcity of time in general, then we experience the sort of anxiety that causes cancer. Who wants to die of cancer! Even with all the medical progress nowadays, this is not a comfortable way to go. Let time be the god-given ambience of your existence and life. There's no end of it. Time and world without end.

* * *

January 2018

An Irrational Ethic

"Except a man be born of water …"

*

"If I will that he tarry till I come …?"

*

An Irrational Ethic

I behave rationally when my attitude to other beings (not things), whether human or otherwise, is growth-directed, in the sense that what matters to me is development and evolution, both for myself and for others.

I behave unrationally, or absurdly, when I see myself as an organism and not as a being, and when my main aim is to adhere to a status quo of some sort, either individually or politically; in which case I do not grow but act according to fixed principles and received dogmas.

I behave irrationally when my attitude to other beings, whether human or otherwise, is growth-directed, though not in terms of action and passion but of being itself.

*

The main difference between rational and irrational ethical behaviour hinges upon how we go about doing good. It is not until we understand truly ethical behaviour as the doing of good, that both rational and irrational behaviour may be understood as possible and helpfully effective both in their own right. While we think of ethical behaviour merely as morally acceptable under definable circumstances, we will invariably class irrational behaviour as a kind of unreasonable behaviour. However there is more to rational behaviour than adherence to reason. It is perfectly reasonable for us to see to our advantage while causing someone else's disadvantage. It is reasonable, in the accepted modern sense of reason, to do ourselves good that does no one else any good and the reasonable good we do does not necessarily have to have anything to do with our awareness of human growth as perceived in terms of development and evolution. Truly ethical behaviour however will always begin by someone doing good to some other being, thereby doing him- or herself good. Also truly ethical conduct is then understood by us as the care we take of others, mindful of their development towards maturity and their evolution during maturity, even while we ourselves grow.

The difference between unrational and irrational behaviour is therefore of crucial importance because the latter, like rational behaviour, is ethical in the sense of doing ethical good, while the former is not. And when we wish to do ethical good, whether rationally or irrationally, we know that in order to do ourselves some good we must begin by doing it for someone else or for other beings. The fact that the ethical good we do can also be for beings other than human beings helps to define what it means to be truly ethical.

In addition to the growth-orientation and the emphasis on doing good by beginning with some other being rather than ourselves, it might also be helpful to keep in mind right from the start that the truly ethical human being does good first and foremost by personal example and not by trying to instil ethical precepts.

So these three considerations pertain to both rational and irrational ethics.

*

In this essay it is irrational ethics that interests us, especially in comparison to rational ethics. So we have to understand that just as we do not stop being when we do, neither do we entirely stop doing when we concentrate on being. So let us agree that being is also a doing. Or we might point to the effect someone might have insofar as he is in one way or another, while he makes no particular effort to change anything, outwardly.

76

This only makes sense when we have human beings in mind. Those who are caught up in the world and do not mind, or they even chose to be caught up, cannot be said to <u>be</u> in the sense we mean now – in the sense of the **being we have**. Human beings have life. They also have being. In comparison, we might say that a thing is but it has no being.

And of course we may depend on the being we have, precisely because we are for a reason. Namely we are that we are. Our being is raised to the level of awareness. And this is what makes those around us aware of us. This awareness does them good. Their own being is drawn to their attention due to their awareness of us caused by our being that we are.

We are that we are not because it makes us feel good. We actually choose to be that we are for the good of others and therefore also for our own good. One imagines there are those who meditate themselves into a veritable storm for the sheer self-appreciation of it but then this can only do them harm eventually as their nerve system is destroyed and as they become insensitive to their environment or as they can no longer differentiate between themselves and others and lack all sense of personality. We can imagine this and it helps to remind us of what we hope to avoid.

*

Being that we are requires a minimum of effort. That is the doing part of it which eventually guarantees the ethical influence. For the purpose of this essay I am that I am for example, to set an example of it in writing, of which others can make use. I know that I am growing even as I wait for the next sentence to occur to me.

This is something those who are persuaded in the direction of irrational ethics soon learn, that it is not up to them to manipulate the world or to change others in any predetermined way but that the good influence must come from within themselves as they do what they do in a non-laborious fashion. Insofar as creation implies the overcoming of reluctance to change, irrational ethics is not creative but facilitative. In other words one does what one can to let growth happen and to continue as smoothly as possible.

Growth is developmental towards evolution and then it is evolutionary. No being grows automatically. Neither can we make ourselves grow. So good sense demands that we learn to perceive growth-stimuli and growth processes, both in ourselves and in other beings, so that we may cooperate with them. Such cooperation begins with a simple affirmation and ends with some output of evidence of our growth. Whatever the output, its effectiveness will always be of the manner of an easing of human growth.

It is modern to equate the amount of effort put into a work with the eventual usefulness of it. It is modern in the sense of 'critically inhibited' to make a virtue out of 'keeping busy'. You've got to do some thing. Leisure is problematic for the modern individual. It smacks of laziness. This is because he equates surviving and living. He also likes to feel alive, such as during heightened sensations of existence, which always end in damaging others too. The 'adrenalin kick' is the curse of modern 'living'.

As human beings try to distance themselves from the modern, unrational ethic of survival at any cost, they might find that it lies within the domain of their giftedness to adopt the irrational ethic. Many, of course, do. This does not make them popular, mainly because popularity is not really ethical in any sense. It does however make them cheerful, friendly and content. They will be sought out by those who value their companionship on account of the aura of peace they often exude.

I do not mean to suggest that a person who chooses to be ethical in a contemporary rather than in modern fashion has to do so either rationally or irrationally. True, some are born whose life then emphasises one or the other, perhaps to draw our attention to the very possibility of ethical behaviour; this is perhaps the purpose of exceptional talents and gifts. However we are fortunate if we can be, behave and act ethically in the contemporary sense without even being aware of much of a difference between the two.[1]

*

Modern, unrational ethics is, of course, coloured by the modern mind-set. Perhaps we should refresh our memory with respect especially to the crisis in which 'modern man' perpetually finds himself. Modern experience, modern thinking and feeling, modern action and production are not based on faith but defined by anxiety and by all the effort required to hide from the cause of this anxiety. It is really a terrible predicament to be modern, as we all know to some extent, whether we choose to be modern, or struggle to be contemporary, or are safe in the contemporary haven from which we set out and to which we return. To be fair, many of those who have chosen to be modern have not yet become sensitive to the danger in which they find themselves.

Some are born who are quite free of the modern anxiety and who cannot really be described as being in the typically modern state of being, so that even in their youth, while the modern population views them as more or less inconveniently abnormal, they often have a peaceful and emotionally stabilizing ef-

---

[1] My essay Folk Nature is interesting with respect to this point.

fect on those around them who are receptive to this, due usually to their own realisation that not all is well with their modern existence.

Understanding and compassion for those who are trapped in the modern mind-set helps us work out our irrational ethic against the backdrop of the modern environment and also in view of the degree to which we ourselves have been influenced by modernity. We may have modern habits of thought, of mental and emotional behaviour, that at times cause us difficulties as we try to grow in a contemporary fashion. We will struggle with setbacks, with all the pain due to wrong decisions based on faulty interpretations of our conditions and circumstances. Our progress often seems too slow and not sufficiently thorough and permanent. The more we understand what it means to be modern, the less likely will we be to lose courage or to remain down when we have fallen.

So for example we know how speeding in our car can give us a heightened sense of self. We 'feel more alive'. We also realize that speeding can be dangerous. So we struggle with the problem of how to prevent ourselves from time and again giving in to this unfortunate habit. We have been given the aid, by our civic authorities, of appropriate speed limits, but how often do we really choose to understand them as beneficial rather than feeling that they are annoying hindrances as we once again exceed the limit by driving 'as fast as we can get away with'. It is evidently something within ourselves that needs to be seen to.

This is where the irrational ethic comes in handy. We deal with the agitation, with the contradictory mental processes inside ourselves, by 'being that we are'. We allow ourselves to sink into our sense of human being. We become so patient within ourselves that we can describe it as a 'tarrying', as a waiting for good sense and awareness to arrive. We allow ourselves to become contemporary. We make no effort at all to go against, to deny or negate, the bad tendency that is our modern, always potentially dangerous, psyche as we lower ourselves into our faithful being. We know our faithful being not as a state in which we need to hold out until some good effect is reached – no, that is not it at all. Rather we know it as the ethical way to be that guarantees our contemporary peace and liveliness.

Our reason for behaving like this is not primarily so that we do not come to grief, but rather so that we do not cause anyone else grief. An irrationally ethical human being considers the other drivers, the pedestrians, cyclists and of course their, and his, relations and friends who would all be inconvenienced if he hurt anyone and for whom a death would cause hardship and grief. And of course he knows that the best he can do for himself is to care for all those others. The one who goes by appearances will say: You only care for me so as to care for yourself. This is blatant nonsense, because one could not possibly care for anyone in a genuine way with such a superficial thought in mind. And what I have described as the very kernel of irrationally ethical behaviour, this immersing ourselves in our being in that certain way, is surely the exact opposite of superficial behaviour.

We may be that we are. We may choose to be for the purpose of being and so that we have being, human being in particular. When I am that I am, I am performing a perfectly reasonable task. It is quite possible for us to hide our being, to conceal the fact that we are, such as when we play a role either to entertain or to deceive. Equally we might lose our being by allowing ourselves to get carried away by thoughtless activity and careless business, such as by giving ourselves to indulgence in virtual reality. All such possibilities are not ethical in

81

any way because we would be entirely preoccupied with our own affairs, perhaps egotistically. Not until we make ourselves aware of the fact that we are on earth primarily for others and only secondarily for ourselves can we begin to comprehend the various ethical moves that one by one will become available to us, through practice of thought and deed.

*

Neither in the case of rational or irrational ethical behaviour do we choose to have anything to do with things but always with being and beings. So we do well to learn the difference. We live in a world that is itself a thing and those who are part of it make things their business. It would be difficult to imagine how we could avoid being affected by things. Neither should we wish to be unaffected by them. It is enough that we do not seek them out. When we are affected by thing-values, we notice this soon enough by the way we tend to react without responding. Any thing-culture after all is a system of reactions, not of response. So we may choose to notice that we tend to react. The we may choose to understand that any such reaction is to be the sign for us that we may now, and would be wise to, respond, ethically; rationally or irrationally. Very likely we are more accustomed to the one than to the other. For the sake of our study here we may observe that a rational ethical response to a modern reaction is outwardly creative in the sense that we utilize, as it were, the reactionary experience as we give shape to some recognizable response that will be of benefit to anyone who would wonder how that sort of behaviour works, or who might even be persuaded for the first time to take courage when modern reactions crowd his soul. In other words, we would produce a work, or create something of value, out of our negative experience. This work might be something we say, even a gesture, a helpful hint to someone who might be afraid of us or a friendly remark to someone who hates us. It might be

82

an essay or a symphony. I want to emphasize this, that a creative work in such a case might be as small as a facial gesture or as large as an epic poem or the construction of a new wing to the local hospital. What gives the work the ethical value is that it embodies a response to a modern reaction.

And if it should occur to anyone, before we go on to compare the irrationally ethical response, that by our response we are able to cause anyone to lay aside his unethical or modern-ethical behaviour, let him instead lay that thought aside. If merciful good spirit does not persuade anyone to behave in a truly ethical fashion, then we ourselves are the sole beneficiaries of our ethical behaviour. We set the example and the other one will benefit from it or not. If he does not, this does not in any way diminish what we ourselves gain from having behaved as we did. The rationally ethical work, however small or great, cannot be lost. The sum-total of good human/divine spirituality/reality grows with every truly ethical act and is ever available to all who take the trouble to develop and evolve.

An irrationally ethical response to modern reaction now can be described as inward rather than outward creation. I do believe that this a useful way to compare the two. What we create inwardly in such a way is our manifold human being.

At this stage I should perhaps emphasize what is in danger of being overlooked in any modern environment, which is that in the case of truly ethical behaviour, the creativity, whether inward or outward, is not first available to ourselves and then to the other one, nor the other way around, but the two moves, or potencies, are contemporary. They are one in time. As we choose to observe them they appear simultaneous and if we choose to speak or write about them they will appear to be two. We may understand that this cannot be otherwise and in the meantime we may remind ourselves now and again of the difference between seeming and being. We have two eyes, two ears, two hands and feet. We even have two brains, in a way. This is the way we are made and there is good reason for it. Surprisingly it fits the way we live and where we exist. We may inspect the front and the back of an apple without forgetting that we hold a single apple.

*

Inward creation increases – and empowers – our human being. By way of our human being – as human beings, more and more effective due to our ethical behaviour – we present ourselves to other beings. We communicate. Our means of communication is language and there are different types of language. What matters for us here, insofar as we are trying to understand irrationally ethical behaviour, is that our own spirit, however rich or poor, and the one that is merciful good spirit are indistinguishable during inward creation.

Is it important for us to know this? It all depends on the extent to which we are called upon to exercise our ethical empowerment. Under different circumstances we come up against different challenges of various degrees and experience soon teaches an active human being that he or she is not for long allowed to take his or her peace of mind for granted.

So first we might ask ourselves: are we aware of ourselves as endowed with spirit? Does that mean anything to us, to be endowed with spirit? Well, we know what it means to be in high spirits or in low spirits. We might also know what it means to be in control of ourselves, to have far-reaching plans and ambitions for ourselves and others, to feel that we can achieve anything if we just put our mind to it and don't let circumstances get us down – and so on. Those who remind the children in their care that they can 'achieve whatever they want, if they just work hard enough' are usually themselves essentially fictional functionaries who cannot be held responsible for what they say.

For the ancients, humans and the gods were involved with each other. Even ancient monotheism left people free to indulge themselves in any degree and type of mythological relationship with their God. Not until modern times – and the plural of 'time' is telling – does human spirit come to stand alone, distinct and discrete from divine spirit – and quite possibly out of range from it. In other words, for two-thousand years now the modern possibility of the demonic person exists. Such a person discovers that in his own way – we might say 'in his own god-forsaken way' as long as we remember that we forsake god and not god us – and entirely within the confines and liberties of his own human spirit, he is able to envision the most magnificent achievements that will astonish the popular world.

Those who turn to god are not astonished by these achievements. They make us feel uneasy, they way we feel uneasy when we see a child climb out on the branch of a tree to retrieve his kite. Only those to whom it is given to distinguish between the spirit that is god and the human spirit, in the same way as they distinguish between their soul and psyche, have the choice to turn to god as merciful good spirit of love. Whenever they specifically choose to so, they are inwardly creative.

We who have the choice to turn to god are at the same time at perfect liberty not to do so – and then, to the extent that we give reign to our own spirit, we become demonic. Instead of making the two one, we allow the one to become two; instead of joining our own spirit to divine spirit, we allow our own spirit to become doubtful and critical. More precisely, our spirit is now either doubtful or critical, and in either case the duality is at work that characterizes the modern tragedy. We call it the tragedy because whether in doubt or critical, modern man is divided in himself and we observe his pitiful struggle to mend himself by means of his own spirit – which itself causes this secondary division.

What shall we do when we see that once again we have become modern?

Oh, nothing could be simpler. We turn to god. Ah, but where is that god? Modern man has little notion of god. He has inadvertently erected so many barriers between himself and god that as soon as he notices his predicament he struggles awfully and he is in dire straits. He is lost and mercifully he knows it.

I am describing what happens when we become modern even though we had what it takes not to become modern. We cannot concern ourselves with those who are modern and they are just fine with that. The deliberations of those who are genuinely lost centre upon the terrible and terrifying distance between themselves and god. We may even have forgotten that once, at least as children, this disconcerting duality did not exist for us. We are depressed or we digress. Whether we think of our depression as self-caused or brought on by circumstances makes not difference to how we are. Whether we digress in the direction of self-harming or harming others, this makes no difference to the fact that we digress. Is there no hope for us? We are not modern because we want to be modern but because we cannot find our way back out of modernity.

As you would expect, there are two ways out of our predicament. Both are irrationally ethical. One way is that we recognize the way we feel. The other is that we acknowledge the way we are. As soon as we genuinely acknowledge for long enough that we can no longer manage by means of our human spirit alone, divine spirit comes to our aid. As soon as we seriously recognize clearly enough that we cannot change the way we feel by means of our solitary human spirit, divine spirit appears on the horizon.

The ethical creativity hinges upon the 'clearly enough' and the 'long enough' and its success depends upon the seriousness and the genuineness of ourselves. We are human beings and though we may be lost, we always have within us the human nature with which we were born. This is not just nature but human nature. No matter how lost we are or how far we have drifted from the spirit that is merciful love, our birthright remains intact. Knowing this, recalling it to mind and actively believing it helps of course. However this will remain for us a vain opinion unless we, at the same time, do the ethically creative work of recognition or acknowledgment. One of these suffices. We may pick the one we prefer. Either one implies a turning away from our solitary human spirit, indeed from our customary will and intellect, as we 'confess' our 'spiritual bankruptcy'.

I cannot myself see how such a confession can ever be other than on our knees, in tears, in our little chamber. Also I would encourage an awareness of the difference between the first time, when we realize once and for all time that not all is lost, and times afterwards, when we have taken it upon ourselves to pass on the good news, to behave in such a way that others might benefit from what we have learned – and due to our exposure it happens that we now and again overreach ourselves or underestimate our potential. It takes time and much practice to learn how to behave ethically and when we practice irrational ethics we are liable to incur some characteristic setbacks. For but one example, we will not be praised for our efforts. Since in reality it is not even expedient for us to make any effort in the first place, this setback, like all the others we are liable to incur, will soon enough be revealed to us as a blessing in disguise. Another apparent setback, along the same lines, is the one that causes us to suppose that time and again we fail because we have not applied ourselves in the right way. How exactly have we failed? Did we know the way to the goal we were able to predict? No, of course not. The road took a turn and we had made up our mind it should go straight.

So with every irrationally ethical move we make we are wise to take in stride that we are in good company, that we cooperate rather than striking out on our own and that we are not here on earth to please ourselves but primarily for the benefit of others – and what a great pleasure it is to succeed at that!

*

Rationally ethical behaviour is creative outwardly, we said, and for the sake of comparison we shall say a few words about it.

No man can be outwardly effective unless he is inwardly sound. By comparison and contrast, anything we do externally or outside is right from the beginning not in touch with our human being and we know human being as being affective and effective, inwardly and outwardly, but not externally or internally. So what we do outwardly is not extinct but live and based on our human being and on our human nature, both of which are based on elementary faith as our human natural foundation.

When we are creative outwardly we are overcoming something that endangers our inward human being. First we recognize that danger and then we decide to turn it into a productive impulse. We feel we are being insulted, so we call to mind that we are either being told the truth, in which case we would better pay heed, or else we are not being told the truth, so we do well to suffer the pain of the insult. It helps if we know that when we suffer such pain we gain in power. Such knowledge should really be part of every outward creative act. We overcome something which is reluctant to be overcome and we perceive it as originating from without us. Always the creativity annihilates any desire for revenge. We are no longer tempted to react, to some person or to circumstances, as it were 'to get our own back'. 'Our own' is powerful human nature and the only way we get that back is by forgiving. We are smart to try to get back to it, by forgiving, as soon as possible, so that we may gain the increase that is our due. If we give in to the temptation to be modern, we will care more about our status, our self-respect, our social standing, in other words our notion we have of ourselves as existing in the eyes of the world. In that case we look for some propitiatory sacrifice, either in the past or at present, or even for a scapegoat.

Our entire life's work might be mainly outwardly creative. Our works will be outwardly perceived by others. What is perceived – by those who do perceive – is that our work is, at the same time, truthful and inwardly based on human natural faith. Mainly we are active so as to overcome a tendency to be inactive and we are creative to overcome a tendency to be destructive. The outwardly creative person keeps in mind that he has within him a repository of reactive material and while he knows that this is not avoidable, he strives at the same time to perpetuate his human nature in some product that is materially available. This is something additional to what he would otherwise achieve inwardly.

So outward creation overcomes the reluctance of stuff and matter to be shaped, while outward ethical creation results in a shape that illustrates or reflects the cooperational human/divine spirit. Nothing is achieved by 'tarrying' but by 'following'. What we follow is the human/divine spirit. We should not suppose that this is necessarily simple and straightforward. All our inward being is enlisted in the interest of outward doing. There is never a shortage of material resistance, and usually we feel this. Nonetheless we do not engage with this as though it were a feeling. It is simply a sign that we are on the right track. We may persist as long as we like. We may even rest in this spirit. This is difficult to believe at first. As an unfortunate consequence we are liable to overexert ourselves or to tire ourselves out. When we find we have done this, we do well to rest and to learn that a measure of progress is good (ethical) while extreme progress is actually regress and not ethical. Regression is nonetheless useful at times, such as when we have to 'unlearn' a lot that has been drummed into us in our youth, when we were not so much brought up as brought to heel within modern circumstances. Works of regression are not ethical, but they are not unethical either, because in no way do they interfere with the world or bring popular morality into disrepute. In other words, the status quo is not diminished or threatened by them.

Perhaps we have a sense now of how following the human/divine spirit differs from waiting for it. We wait for it within ourselves because we know what the ambition of this spirit is, namely to give us what is good and true and beautiful once we are suitably receptive and in a position to pass it on, while the passing on of it and the making of it available does not involve the overcoming of any reluctant matter within ourselves but is mostly like a childlike offering.

*

Nothing makes much sense unless we have some notion of what it means to be a human being. The passage from humanity through human being to finally a human being – what could be more exciting, more fraught with exposure to the elements, my modern friends? Let us altogether undertake the journey. It will get very warm after a while and then very cold before recognition is drawn down upon us by our irrationally ethical manner of progress. We shall not rush ahead of the spirit that feeds and informs. A measured pace is recommended and a sharp eye out for any loose change.

Humanity, then, is to be imagined as a huge pool, a primordial soup full of all the goodies that must eventually populate the good old universe whether it likes it or not. This liquid concoction, this fantastic brew, this origin of all that is good and true and beautiful – what shall we call it now? We call it humanity. I thought we had decided that.

Under a rock very close nearby – a crystal! No one has ever seen it. How did it get there? No one knows. This is ever so important, that we confess, in the nobility of our character, what we just simply do not know. It is not an oversight that we do not know, but an ethical decision. Good will moves me to share that with you, my dear modern companion. We children of the contemporary spirit are chosen to choose what we know and what we do not know – what we do not subject to our knower. Soon you will be able to grasp that, as you journey with me along this road. We are not in the grip of knowledge, fastened to it by chains of epistemological steel, no, we decide what to know and what not to know. And what we reject today we may take up tomorrow, or vice versa. Our knowing is delicate, aristocratic, refined. We are choosy knowers. Enough said, we do not know something merely because it can be known. So we do not know, at least not just at the moment, how that crystal got there.

What we do know is that a gust of wind budged that stone aside and a drop of the primordial brew landed on that crystal – whereupon it breathed. Oh wonder upon wonders! Look, tiny lines criss-cross everywhere. That which was a mere thing is no longer a thing but it is itself, nothing else. Was it tired of being a thing? Did it chafe at the thought that a thing has no being? Perhaps. That is a thing. Look at that thing, we say, and god gives us a slap on the wrist. How can something be a thing. Things are not. They have no being. Granted? We shall henceforth ignore them. If someone buys us a bucketful for Christmas, well, no need to be a boor, thank you very much, that's lovely, oh, look at those, where did you buy those? We might even enjoy a little paddle in the pool of that hypnotic hypocrisy that quietens the popular mind. As we mentioned earlier, a little regression at times is unavoidable and not at bottom a shameful thing.

A drop of the brew lands smack on that crystal and now it is. Now it is a crystal. 'Behold! Accost! Front her, board her, woo her, Sir Andrew.'[1] For now she has being. The crystal is. We make no further demands on her but we allow her space and time to develop. There's the very charm of life in that, I say. Oh to be touched by humanity! Can it happen to just anyone? Might it happen to you, my friend, in your modern armour of pictorial images and impersonal precepts? We'll come back to that.

Is it true then that we are born into this pool of being? Are we suddenly human-natural? And before, what were we? Ancient? Modern? What exactly does it mean to be born? I choose to know this. It means to be set adrift on the pool of humanity, which is being. I, personally, would much rather be than not be and I do not apologize for mentioning that. I am born; I have birth. Or: I am borne, I have berth. I insist on the latter. I have human nature visited upon me. I may from now on take the fullest possible advantage of the fact that I am borne. For sure, I would be foolish not to. Why am I borne after all? Is it to en-

---

[1] In casual reference: Sir Toby to Sir Andrew in 'Twelfth Night.'

tertain those who are not yet borne? No, let them entertain themselves; they have their stand-up comics, by the gross, sir! I regress. They have their unconscious self-appeal and their post-graduate courses in how to make friends and influence people. Basta!

A drop of humanity is all it takes. Suddenly our human nature is revealed to us. We are no longer modern but susceptible to the drops of gold that rain down from on high. Momentarily we want to be drenched and that is understandable. The rain stops and a hot, yellow light burns us to a crisp. This too makes sense, for we are to learn now what it means to have human being and to be in the possession of our human nature, of this gift of the one and only god who makes his home within us now. So we hold out in the heat. You may stand in my shade if you like, I am used to this. I come here periodically to refresh my memory. Yes, I know, it's hell the first time. But cheer up. Take it as a sign of the fact that you are blessed and that the goods are on the way – if you hold out.

Now I must warn you, if you keep complaining it will not go well with you. I would advise you strongly against what you are doing now. There is nothing to be gained from finding fault with your condition. You say you want to write a paper on the effects of sunlight on the moods and manners of a desiccated man, for recognition by the Smithsonian in Washington? I have my doubts.

I am human. I have human being. So much so good. I count my blessings. However I am not there yet. I circle around that pool like someone who contemplates his navel. In short, I must find something to do. Why is that, I wonder. Why do rather than not do? Why not sleep?

In short, I cannot sleep. Nightmares wake me. I try to sleep; now and again I turn my face to the wall and close my eyes just to prove to the world and to my lesser nature that they will not let me sleep, these upheavals in the dark. Their luminescent outlines define them as toxic. They indulge in rumours, they make unfair accusations and try to sell their sexual favours to politicians from the underground. I sense real danger. Am I to lose my being again? Is my human nature to be ripped out of me by those who insist there is no such thing in the first place?

This is evil. I must do something. I must do something good. It's high time. Time to be ethical. No, to do ethical. It appears I have two choices. That may be mere appearance but let me see how it works. I can retreat into my human nature and say to all this evil: Do your worst! That will keep me awake. Beyond that I will be setting a valuable example for those who keep turning over and over, in turns fascinated by their nightmares and wishing they were rid of them; making a fuss about them at the dinner table, complaining about them on the streets, concocting dissertations about them at the university. I will withdraw into my human nature and maybe sing a song or two, to advertise my contentment. That's clever enough but let's face it, it's not really good. I shrink from myself after a while. I am being dishonest, ungrateful, disingenuous. I have a hunch that I am capable of more and better. I know what's going on. I am being infected by the condition of those who are affected by evil. Now I have my real work cut out for me. In short I am faced with the need to become a human being. I certainly don't want to continue to fester, with a lower and lower opinion of myself as someone who is too full of himself to recognize his comparative emptiness and do something about it. Don't ask me to identify cause and effect here; I don't see it like that and that is not how it is. Somehow I have to learn how to deal with this infection of myself. Oh don't get me wrong, I do feel like castigating that lot who cause me this trouble – except that of course they don't. No, I'll have none of this cause and effect pusillanimity.

94

Even though the evil is no longer outside me but inside me now, I will nonetheless insist on my human nature in the very face of this nausea, this threat of disintegration – this despair.

I am singing a different song now. Oh yes, my song is confirming human nature in the presence of the thing that would annihilate it – at least that is how I see it, and I highly suspect that that is how it is. My human nature, the very spirit that is Jesus in god, gives me courage and says: Come to me and I will set you free. That is what my song amounts to, in one version or another. I know I am not on my own. My modern friend is still busy with his dissertation. He is proving beyond the shadow of a doubt that there is no such thing as evil. If that satisfies him, who am I to say nay?

By immersing myself in my human being I become an actual human being; an ethical being. By confirming that my human nature is endowed with good spirit I simply annihilate the duplicity of the infection. This confirmation is my real work. And believe me, while I exist in the modern world and neither hide from it nor fight it, there is no end of need for confirmation.

Now mind you, if the modern world no longer existed for one reason or another, I would not be lost for words. Evil is not necessary for me to be a fully fledged human being. I would be quite happy 'being like one of the angels', don't you know. Not an angel, take note, but like one. Big difference.

*

Again, how is it creative what I do when I circumvent evil. I certainly don't resist it. Which is not to say I do not find it abhorrent, disgusting, terrifying, boring, irritating, and sometimes just plain incomprehensible. When I hear of a child being tortured by his parents, apparently for the sheer pleasure they derive from it, I feel so angry I could jump out of my skin. When

95

I read that the leaders of various nations behave like benighted psychopaths I sink into despair. Now however the work begins. In the presence, in oneself, of despair, for one example, one can go wrong basically in two opposite ways, both of which are not creative. One can say to oneself: 'Well, what do you expect. The world is an evil place.' That way the despair is lost on us. Or one can say: 'I must let out my despair on someone or something. I must speak in a despairing manner so that my emotion is externalized, and therefore someone else's burden.'

If instead I want to make something good of it, something that will replace it in some manner or form, I must let the despair work itself out in me. This is possible only if my human nature is intact, if I am in the possession of my soul and if I know therefore that evil cannot harm me. Initially of course I react and feel the despair as if I were the cause of it and must quickly justify myself because I am not. My reaction is a case of my judging so that I will not be judged. The human side of me reacts like this and if I were merely human, I would in fact empower my reaction, indulge in a bout of lively self-justification and find someone to blame whom I would perhaps scorn from then on.

However I am also divine. I am not merely human, but human/divine. It is 'only human', as we are told often enough, to react and to energize our reaction intentionally. We are told this not as a reproach, which would make ethical sense, but as an excuse and usually we are glad for it and comforted. Cheap comfort indeed. Especially cheap since the adjective human does itself in reality embrace an equal human dimension. Even this, that we feel we have to say: 'We are not only human but also divine', is a sign of modernity and only on the way to the truth.

So perhaps we can get used to saying that we are human, not merely human, and take it for granted that some will know what we mean, namely that humanity is godly and god is humanly.

In the light, then, of our being growth-oriented and given that we intend to behave ethically, we may describe our inward creativity as a substituting of good for evil. Not that a description ever convinced anyone to emulate. If we have succeeded once or twice in being inwardly creative we will at least realize how long it will probably take before we will have made a habit of it. It can literally take years. Again and again we supply our reactions with oxygen. However it takes but once for us to regret this and we can say we have evidence of the fact that we are not born to die.

If we know our human nature as the domain of the resurrected Jesus, then our inward creativity will have that extra personal dimension that comes with religious piety. The regression that would be necessary, however, for most moderns, before they could truly think in those terms without falling away into superstition and magic, seems almost too much to ask. Neither is Jesus of Nazareth merely a historic personage or a myth. Thankfully creative philosophy can prepare us for the ethical task in hand because the creative philosopher will be aware how god has adjusted reality through Jesus and how there is no going back to a lesser version of it. Eventually we may even be able to understand our own development and evolution as our resurrection from among the dead, or perhaps we should say 'from among the moderns'. Eventually then the Gospels will begin to make proper sense to us and we will no longer use them as prayer wheels or as a collection of mantras.

*

For those who are acquainted with the Jesus of the Gospels and with the reality of the resurrected Jesus within themselves, there are times when it suffices for them to think: 'I follow' or to feel 'I tarry', and the work proceeds or gets done. How can this not be a marvellous message, when we want to be free to participate even among those whose wits have forsaken them or whose pride has misled them! 'Tarry' we feel and within us the moment is floodlit with faith surpassing all sense and sensibility, with belief so most reasonably masculine or feminine that mostly we wish we could teach the slaves of their emotions and the servants of their self-esteem this lovely path of inward creativity. What is it that mostly stands in the way? An entirely wrong attitude to the childlike simplicity with which we can manage our most important affairs. We are far too adult, perhaps too engrained in our adultery, to understand readily that our mature humanity waits for us just around the corner as our acceptance of merciful good spirit of love into ourselves as our soul.

Our irrationally ethical soul – what does it really amount to? Much has been said about 'soul' that brings tears to our eyes for the lack of informed compassion. It cannot be for those who glory in their psyche to comfort us in our soulless state. And yet we are reminded by our psyche that in the absence of our soul we are depressed and distressed. We can no longer make ourselves out on the human horizon. We strive and struggle and strut our stuff light-years beyond where our god would share with us his joy with his creation. What are we doing out there, diminished to a point? The utter loneliness of the human heart deprived of its natural disposition to community needs to be shared.

* *

98

'We behave irrationally when our attitude to other beings, whether human or otherwise, is growth-directed, though not in terms of action and passion but of being itself.'

That was our definition of irrational behaviour at the beginning of this essay. We are growth-directed in the sense that we organize ourselves, discipline ourselves, dedicate and devote ourselves in a manner that takes the fullest possible advantage of all that has been truthfully achieved for the purpose of enabling us to empower ourselves as mature human beings. That is half the definition. Growth-orientation, even as in the case of a more rational ethic, involves an ongoing proving and disproving of ourselves in the light of a greater reality that is not produced or invented by ourselves, however worthily in union, but ever available to us providentially while we learn and work to be of benefit to one another.

The definition of ethical behaviour more specifically irrational draws us into the realm of being, of human being first and foremost, within which we become progressively aware of our relation to all other beings and therefore of our responsibility for highlighting such relationships proevidentially and exemplifying them within our own being.

*

Both rational and irrational ethics are creative. We may tend to believe that action is useful exclusively inasmuch as we 'act upon' this or that, as we bring about beneficial change. Out here in world-environment, in the light of day, we calculate likely results and weigh consequences as we bring our creative love to bear on that environment. Of course we are able to do good out here only to the extent that we are inwardly soundly based on elementary faith. At the same time we do well not to ignore what those who are more inwardly gifted are able to achieve on our behalf. Undeniably under the influence of the lively environment in which they find themselves, they have what it takes to set merciful and compassionate examples of essential humanity, of definitive human being and of human personality that is bound to inspire and recreate us. How they go about this has more to do with how they are (being that they are) than with what they do. It is their personal disposition that influences us, as it changes from one moment to the next, not so much anything they intentionally activate or produce. It is as if human nature (this human/divine nature!) were saying to us: 'Even I myself, irrespective of any of your wishes and desires, know what is good for your community and for your development and evolution within that community.' The irrationally ethical one is creative in that he chooses to make room for, to facilitate, human/divine nature so that it becomes more thoroughly his and then ours. He overcomes his reluctance not to do so. Why might he be reluctant? Mostly on account of another onset of self-satisfaction. His nature reminds him, nudges him. Suddenly he is in a mood. He becomes cranky, aggressive, sickly: 'What's wrong with me today?' is the start of his creative insight. He once again chooses to be that he is and ends by potentially influencing positively our development and growth.

*

Reality over the past two-thousand years, wherever it has not been undermined by the modern rehearsal of grief or overruled by the modern insistence on criticism, shows us itself as both rationally and irrationally ethical due to those human beings who have laid down their life for others. It is with justice that we describe ethical behaviour as a laying down of one's life for others. This description holds for both rational and irrational ethics. In both ways we do good, whether actively or passively, intentionally or graciously, with an eye to making life on earth, for human beings and therefore for all be-ings, as perfect as our father in heaven.

* * * * *

Traumear, January, 2018

www.ingramcontent.com/pod-product-compliance
Lightning Source LLC
Chambersburg PA
CBHW060416290526
45791CB00002B/773